THE DEAD BELOW

Also by Richard Estep

In Search of the Paranormal
Haunted Longmont
The World's Most Haunted Hospitals
Visiting the Ghost Ward
Trail of Terror
Colorado UFOs
The Devil's Coming to Get Me
The Fairfield Haunting
Haunted Healthcare
The Horrors of Fox Hollow Farm

As co-author

The Haunting of Asylum 49
Spirits of the Cage

The Dead Below

The Haunting of Denver Botanic Gardens

Richard Estep

In loving memory of

Chuck Hicks *and* ***Brianna Harlow***

Two of the finest EMTs I ever knew.

The afterlife just gained one heck of an ambulance crew.

Clear skies.

I miss you.

Contents

Introduction
1. The Bones of Mount Calvary
2. "...many coffins have not been moved."
3. Ghosts in the Gardens
4. "I Have Never Been More Terrified in My Life..."
5. Get Me Out of Here
6. "In the Name of the Father..."
7. "Get Out!"
8. "IN A MASS GRAVE"
9. Demon
10. The Devil's Toybox
11. Roses
12. Just Shut Up
13. We Saw Her
Afterword
Acknowledgments

Introduction

The movie *Poltergeist* is a true Hollywood classic, and deservedly so. After all, what's not to love? Creepy old trees that come alive in the night, objects whizzing around the house at breakneck speed, and ghosts coming out of a staticky TV set are just some of the highlights offered up in Steven Spielberg and Tobe Hooper's 1982 genre masterpiece.

Poltergeist is also an eminently quotable movie, and never more so than the scene in which Steven, the head of the tormented Freeling family (played by Craig T. Nelson) confronts his penny-pinching bureaucratic weasel of a boss and demands to know why there are coffins exploding out of the ground outside his home, dumping skeletal human remains in all directions.

"You son of a bitch! You moved the cemetery, but you left the bodies, didn't you?! *You only moved the headstones!* Why? **WHY?!?"**

This point in the movie's finale is one of the things that practically *everybody* remembers about it, even if they haven't seen the movie in years. For some reason, the concept of a graveyard relocation in which the headstones were removed, and yet the bodies were not, seems to hold an eerie fascination for us, a grisly piece of urban folklore that sits right alongside those stories of houses that were built on top of an ancient Native American burial ground.

But all of this is just myth, the macabre imagination of a Hollywood screenwriter at work...isn't it?

Surprisingly, a cursory flip through the history books reveals that this has happened far more often than one would like to think.

Ask practically any Denver resident (and pretty much any Coloradoan) about Cheesman park, and they'll tell you a variation of the same tale: how the City of Denver once took a major cemetery that was somewhat the worse for wear, and paid a shady private contractor to relocate those who were buried there. He, in turn, made a half-hearted effort to exhume some — but not all — of those bodies, and then re-inter them in another graveyard, this one further away from the general population.

The reason that is often given for the vast majority of the bodies were simply left in their original graves was the greed and ineptitude of the contractor who was chosen by the city to carry out this grim task — though as we shall see, this may not be entirely fair. When stories began to circulate of multiple bodies being stuffed into the same coffin, and of skeletons being smashed and broken in order to make them fit, a scandal duly ensued and a public outcry arose. The graves — now devoid of headstones — were then filled in, landscaped over, and the authorities hoped that the whole fracas would simply blow over.

What cannot be denied is the fact that anybody who walks in Cheesman Park and its surrounding areas today, is walking on top of hundreds, if not thousands, of sets of human remains.

Although some parts of this oft-told tale have become a little overblown, the core of the story contains more than just a kernel of actual truth.

One thing is for certain. The Cheesman Park area is steeped in history, not all of which is pleasant. Where there is history, one also tends to find ghosts.

I have been a paranormal investigator for the past twenty-four years at the time of writing, and an author working in the same field for the past five of those. When I first came to the United States in 1999 (having relocated from my native Great Britain) I heard the same stories concerning Cheesman

Park, filed them away in a part of my brain labelled, *that's interesting, must follow up on that sometime,* and then went on about my business.

Accounts of people having ghostly experiences in the park and its surrounding environs continued to circulate within the paranormal research community, but I really didn't give the place much thought for the next seventeen years or so.

Fast-forward to 2016, more specifically a few days after Halloween. I make my living as a paramedic. My boss, a no-nonsense chief paramedic named Chris, had little time for ghost stories. He was well aware of my side interest, and was polite enough to refrain from saying that he thought it was a pretty dubious subject. Once, after reading a book I had written about ghosts and their connection to the Gettysburg campaign, he diplomatically told me, "I liked the history parts a lot more than the ghost parts."

The man could give lessons in diplomacy.

Which made it all the more surprising when he came into the office early one morning and told me that I really ought to check out the ghosts at Denver Botanic Gardens. When I asked him why, he explained that his sister-in-law had just taken a ghost tour there, and that the tour guide had told them some pretty hair-raising stories about the place being haunted.

Supposedly, one of the night security guards had fled the building halfway through his shift, swearing that he would never set foot in the building ever again after what he had experienced that night. (In all fairness to the poor man, he really *was* working 'graveyard' shifts, in more ways than one…)

After spending the day mulling it over, I finally decided to reach out to the leadership team at the botanic gardens. After all, nothing ventured, nothing gained, right?

To my great surprise, they actually seemed quite interested in the idea of a book being researched and written about the haunting of the botanic gardens and their surrounding environs. A few days later, I visited the facility's administrative headquarters, located at the beautiful and historic Waring House (of which much more shall be said later).

I was fortunate enough to be given an impromptu tour of this grand old house, and afforded the opportunity to speak with management and staff members alike. Some, though by no means all of them had their own spooky stories to share about their time working at the botanic gardens, and their experiences ranged all the way from the simple and readily explainable ("I always have a very bad, creeped-out feeling in this one particular spot") to the genuinely befuddling, such as the employee who reported hearing voices in the empty building that told them in no uncertain terms to "get out!"

When the director asked about the requirements of researching and writing such a book, I explained that I would need access to the botanic gardens for the duration of several nights, so that my team could conduct an investigation into the alleged paranormal activity. I told him that if nothing happened, there would be no book. It was as simple as that. I wasn't interested in making a mountain out of a molehill, a position that he seemed to find reassuring.

I am the founder and current director of the Boulder County Paranormal Research Society (BCPRS), an organization of like-minded individuals who spend much of our free time investigating claims of paranormal activity in various forms. Our ranks are diverse, staffed by medical professionals and engineers, information technology specialists and mechanics, and pretty much anything and everything in between. We all have one thing in common, however: a shared desire to get to the truth of these mysteries, no matter what that truth may be. Quite often we find a completely mundane, everyday explanation, but in other cases, we encounter things that seem genuinely inexplicable.

After some deliberation, the director agreed to my request, on the condition that certain areas of the premises were to be kept strictly off-limits: primarily some of the offices in the Waring House, the administrative center of the botanic gardens, which contained a certain amount of sensitive and proprietary information. I agreed wholeheartedly, considering it a small price to pay for being granted relatively unfettered access to such a beautiful facility and its surroundings.

A number of the staff preferred not to cooperate (or simply had no experiences to share), which I certainly respected, but others came forward willingly and shared some of their more perplexing workplace experiences with me. You will read about those events later on in this book. It's safe to say that some of them may have perfectly natural explanations, whereas others most definitely do not...

One staff member flatly refuses to stay at her desk after dark, but for the most part, the atmosphere at the botanic gardens is a very warm and friendly one. People seem to very much enjoy working there, from what I could see, and the majority of employees co-exist quite happily with what some believe to be the spirits of those who are buried just a few feet beneath the ground on which they go about their business every day.

Whenever any type of digging is carried out in the areas in and around Denver Botanic Gardens, it is a safe bet that some part of one of the old cemetery's inhabitants will be unearthed.

Sometimes, such discoveries are relatively minor: coffin handles, fragments of wood, brass plaques, and other scraps of burial material have all come out of the ground before. At other times, human remains are unearthed. This may be a small bone such as a finger or toe, but on some occasions entire graves have been discovered, usually still containing their long-dead occupant.

Interviewed by CNN in November of 2010, Jill McGranahan of the city's Parks and Recreation Department spoke candidly about the matter.[1]

"Many of the bodies left in Prospect Cemetery were paupers and criminals," McGranahan said. "Unfortunately, there is no way of knowing or even finding out who they are or if they have existing relatives."

Before contractors are permitted to begin any sort of

work in the area of Cheesman Park that will require digging or excavation, representatives of the city forewarn them about the possibility of disturbing one of the old cemetery's original inhabitants.

"We told them of Cheesman's past and that coming upon skeletons was a real possibility," McGranahan said.

"They all agree that it was still unsettling the first time. As one of our workers stated, he arrives after the sun is up and leaves before it goes down so he doesn't take any chances."

A November 7, 2008 article in the Denver Post is fairly representative of the kind of incidents that still take place to this day. The article by reporter Howard Pankratz, titled *'Old Grave Halts Work at Denver Botanic Gardens'*[2] goes on to tell the story of a grisly discovery made by construction workers who were building a new parking garage on the east side of the botanic gardens, located at 1007 York Street.

Historically, this land was part of Cemetery Hill, and many of Denver's deceased Hebrew community members were buried there, until the final funeral took place in 1903. The Hebrew cemetery was then abandoned, and a good faith effort was made to remove as many of the coffins buried there as possible when the City of Denver purchased the land back again.

Inevitably some of those graves were missed, and it is likely that those were some of the coffins which were unearthed during the construction of the new parking structure, two thirds of which is buried underground for aesthetic purposes.

In the fall of 2008, at the very outset of the construction project, the management team at the botanic gardens strongly suspected that the construction workers would disturb some of those missing graves during the excavation process. They decided to be proactive, and contacted the coroner's office before ground was first broken on the new parking lot. What, they asked, should be done in the event of human remains turning up at the site?

The coroner's instructions were very specific. If the construction crews uncovered anything that resembled a coffin, grave, or skeleton, they were to immediately stop what they were doing and notify the coroner's office without delay. No matter how old the human remains appeared to be, identification of them would be the coroner's responsibility. Only when the authorities were satisfied that this wasn't a crime scene could the bodies be turned over to interment professionals for reburial in a suitable location, which would be a proper cemetery.

And that is precisely what happened in November 2008. A team from the Denver coroner's office came directly to the scene and conducted their own assessment of the newly-discovered body. Once they were satisfied that the industrial digging equipment had unearthed yet another of the former City Cemetery's residents, they removed the bones and allowed construction to recommence. The skeletal remains were treated with all of the dignity and respect that they deserved.

Two years later, in the fall of 2010, a different team of construction workers were excavating on the grounds in order to install a new irrigation system, when they discovered something similar: four human skeletons, all of which were extremely well-preserved.

One is forced to wonder exactly how many other graves still lie beneath the parking structure and under the botanic gardens themselves, perhaps to be discovered at a future date and time…or maybe they will simply lay there forever.

When all was said and done, my team and I spent five nights investigating the Gardens. This book tells the story of that investigation. Although it briefly discusses the history of the property, it is far from an authoritative account — for that, the reader must look elsewhere. (For those who are interested, I heartily recommend the books of Phil Goodstein as a great starting point).

In the field of paranormal research, the answers are rarely cut and dried. In fact, it is safe to say that every answer that is obtained tends to spawn an even greater number of questions, something which paranormal investigators find both maddening and fascinating in equal measure. That was certainly true in this case.

If you do not believe in the existence of ghosts, then this book is unlikely to change your mind…nor is it intended to try and do so. My team and I experienced things that, in our opinion at least, were almost certainly paranormal in nature. But what person A is willing to accept as evidence, person B may find wholly unconvincing. We each set our own bar for proof at a level with which we are comfortable, and when it comes to the subject of ghosts and hauntings, some skeptics refuse to admit that the bar even exists in the first place. No matter what they are presented with, they simply will not believe — and that is certainly their right.

What follows is an honest accounting of our field

investigation. I have done my best to evoke a 'you are right there with us' style, yet the reader is advised that this may present a somewhat distorted view of a day in the life of a paranormal investigator. In reality, ninety percent of our time is spent waiting around for the other ten percent to happen. Now, don't get me wrong: that fantastic ten percent, when it finally *does* happen, makes the other ninety percent more than worthwhile. Make no mistake, however, there is a great deal of boredom and monotony in what we do.

With that being said, nobody wants to read a book in which nothing much is happening, particularly when it is a ghost story. This is a relatively slim volume, in terms of page count. That is because I have taken the liberty of cutting out the hours of interminable waiting around that we all put in while working on this case.

There is an old saying which maintains that drama is life with all of the boring bits taken out. That is as good a definition as any for what I have tried to accomplish with this book, but I must assure the reader that while hours and hours of fruitless waiting have been cut out of the narrative, the events which are described in these pages are all accurately documented to the very best of my ability. I have not exaggerated anything, nor has anything been embellished or made up. Audio recorders were used throughout the majority of our investigation, which meant that our own fallible memories were supplemented by a recorded log of events that helped ensure the accuracy of the manuscript.

If you should happen to find yourself in Denver one day, dear reader, then I encourage you to take a stroll along York Street and visit the botanic gardens for yourself. The plants and flowers are breathtakingly beautiful, the staff are friendly, and the ghosts…well, let's go and meet them, shall we?

Richard Estep
Longmont, Colorado
January 2019

[1] http://www.cnn.com/2010/US/11/18/denver.park.cemetery/index.html

[2] http://www.denverpost.com/2008/11/07/old-grave-halts-work-at-denver-botanic-gardens/

CHAPTER ONE
The Bones of Mount Calvary

There are, broadly speaking, two ways to approach a paranormal field investigation.

One school of thought holds that the investigators should learn as little as possible about the supposedly haunted location before they arrive on-site. Remaining ignorant of the place in which they will be working for the next several days should help to keep them free from contamination and bias, or at least as much as can reasonably be expected. By deliberately choosing not to interview witnesses in advance, identify potential hotspots for paranormal activity, or delve into the backstory of the location, the team can help ensure that they are not unduly influenced or prejudiced. This can be particularly helpful whenever psychics, mediums or sensitives are a part of the investigation.

At the opposite end of the spectrum are those investigators who like to research the location in great depth prior to their visit. Digging into the backstory of a place can shed light on the reasons why it might be haunted in the first place, and collating eyewitness testimony can help pinpoint the best places on which to focus one's investigative efforts.

After all, we are all working on a limited schedule, a finite budget, and only have so many cameras and instruments to deploy. Knowing the best place to put them can help stack the odds in your favor, which is extremely useful when investigating somewhere as big as the botanic gardens. It has a huge physical footprint, and a relatively small team of investigators would find it next to impossible to cover every part of it.

To that end, the first thing I needed to do was hit the library to check some of the public records, and then hit the history books. The story of the haunting of the botanic gardens began long before there ever even *was* a botanic gardens.

As with so many ghost stories, this one began with something abhorrent.

General William Larimer, Jr. is best known as the founding father of the City of Denver. Making a large sum of money as a railroad tycoon, the Pennsylvanian increased his profits exponentially by investing them in land speculation in the booming territory of Kansas. Kansas was good to Larimer; small wonder, then, that when he staked a claim of one square mile close to the South Platte River in November of 1858, he named the fledgling city 'Denver City.'

Needless to say, the governor of Kansas Territory, one James W. Denver, was absolutely delighted.

A nearby settlement named Auraria initially shared some rivalry with Larimer's Denver City, but in less than two years the two competitors had merged, unifying under the name by which the city is still known today: Denver.

The Territory of Colorado was established in 1861. As a key player in setting up the new Territory, Larimer was able to push for Denver to become its capital city. Larimer has a county named after him today, and his influence looms large over the birth and subsequent development of Denver from a relatively minor settlement to a bustling urban metropolis. As miners, pioneers and prospectors made their way west, many chose to settle down in Denver, plying their various trades and raising families in the shadow of the Rocky Mountains.

As Denver grew, so did its need for a cemetery. The second half of the nineteenth century was a dangerous and violent time, with stabbings, shootings, and other crimes of violence being relatively commonplace.

One could also fall from a horse, be run over by a cart,

or suffer one of a thousand different accidental deaths. Although smaller towns might make do with a basic graveyard, a city with aspirations of greatness needed to go one step further and develop a burial ground that it could be proud of.

Larimer picked out the 160-acre plot of land for what would come to be known as the Mount Prospect Cemetery in 1859 (also known as the Prospect Hill Cemetery), taking great care to place it close enough to Denver for it to be convenient, and yet not so close that residents would be constantly reminded of the shadow of death that hung over their fair city.

The first to be interred was a young man named Abraham Kay, who died of an infection on 17th March 1859, and was buried at Mount Prospect three days later. For a 26 year-old to die of a pulmonary condition is almost unheard of today, yet in the nineteenth century such tragedies were commonplace. Kay wouldn't spent long in the ground without company; soon enough the stream of bodies was flowing thick and fast.

On April 7 of that same year, a disagreement between one John Stoefel and his brother-in-law suddenly turned violent. The German immigrant shot his relative dead in cold blood, allegedly in order to procure his stash of gold dust. Both men were gold prospectors by trade, and so the law enforcement officials of the time didn't have to look too far in order to establish a motive.

The closest official court and judge was to be found in Leavenworth, Kansas, but the people of Denver had their blood up and possessed no desire to wait. Judged to be as guilty as sin by a "people's court," Stoefel was duly sentenced to death by hanging: the first such execution ever recorded in the history of Denver, and one carried out in a very timely manner. Just two days after having committed the murder, Stoefel was swinging by the neck from the branches of a cottonwood tree while a huge crowd of cheering spectators looked on.

Displaying a sense of irony that bordered on the perverse, undertakers buried both the murder and his victim in the same coffin on April 9.

Although it soon began to fill up, Mount Prospect never fulfilled William Larimer's hopes for it to become a respectable garden of eternal rest. For one thing, rather than the acres of freshly-manicured lush green lawns that he had at first envisioned, he was dismayed when Mount Prospect proved to look more like a desert dust bowl. There was simply not enough water running close to the cemetery for the land to be irrigable. Weeds ran rampant throughout, although some at least were eaten by the dogs, cattle, and coyotes that wandered about the place, defecating wherever they pleased. Nor were the graves well-tended, and many collapsed in on themselves like sinkholes.

There was no real rhyme or reason for who was buried where. Many families simply interred their loved one wherever they pleased, simply picking a spot and beginning to dig. Whatever else Mount Prospect was, it certainly wasn't aesthetically pleasing.

Eventually, however, a form of haphazard organization began to be imposed on the cemetery, primarily due to the various cultures and religious factions of Denver all wanting their dearly departed to be buried alongside one another. Catholics should be buried alongside Catholics, or so the thinking went; Protestants alongside Protestants; Jews alongside Jews, and so on.

Purchasing a sizable chunk of land, Denver's Catholic community carved out their own niche of real estate for the dead in 1865, naming it the Mount Calvary Cemetery. It is important to remember that this is the ground on which the botanic gardens would one day be situated.

Other faiths followed suit, further segregating Mount Pleasant into several religious territories. Inevitably, there were disagreements and rivalries, and when they started to get out of hand, the U.S. Government itself finally felt the need to put its foot down, annexing the entire cemetery and announcing that it was now federal land.

The residents of Denver were less than thrilled by this turn of events, but could see no better option than to petition the government to sell their own city land back to them. This Uncle Sam graciously agreed to do in 1872, for the princely sum of $200 ($1.25 per acre) on the proviso that it could only ever be used as a cemetery; no residences or city buildings could ever be built there.

In 1876, the Riverside cemetery opened for business. It was nicer than Denver's original cemetery, and attracted a better class of clientele. If you had the money for it, you buried your loved ones in Riverside, not Mount Prospect, which was another reason why the latter began to wither on the vine.

The people of Denver decided that they would quite like a park, and where better than the site of the old cemetery? Lobbying Congress to allow a park to be built in the area where Mount Prospect currently sat, they duly received permission, and as a measure of their gratitude, the future park was to be named Congress Park.

The last burial at Mount Prospect took place in 1893. The powers-that-be determined that the designs for a park were going to be fully implemented, and therefore plans must be made to move the thousands of bodies that lay buried in the now-defunct cemetery.

Moving an entire cemetery's worth of bodies (numbering in the thousands) all the way across the city was a complex and gargantuan undertaking, one that required a great deal of planning, effort, and logistical support if it were to be successful. Investing the necessary time and resources would have been the right and proper thing to do, particularly when one was dealing with something as delicate as the reburial of thousands of dead human beings. As the old saying goes, if a job is worth doing, then it's worth doing right.

Sadly, the job wasn't been done even remotely right.

After winning the contract to relocate the city's dead to the greener pastures of Riverside Cemetery, the Denver-based undertaker Edward McGovern had wasted no time in setting his men to work.

Exhuming hundreds of bodies was hot, unpleasant and sweaty labor, and the men with the shovels weren't being paid particularly well to do it. They cussed and grumbled constantly while they dug. Many wore handkerchiefs tied across their noses and mouths in a vain attempt to keep out the stench. The measure was only marginally successful, and some found themselves gagging and retching when they got a little too close to the object of their work.

From one corner of the cemetery to the other, clusters of men shoveled dirt and soil into untidy heaps. When the tips of their shovels finally struck wood, two of them would haul the newly-unearthed coffin out of its grave and up into the glaring sunlight.

Coffins were strewn everywhere, most of them in various states of damage and disrepair. Whispers began to circulate among the citizens of Denver that the man who had been awarded the contract of overseeing the relocation of the cemetery residents was more interested in making a quick buck than in affording the dead the dignity and respect that should have been their due. The workmen in his employ were, the rumors said. not above stuffing several sets of human remains into a single coffin, breaking bones where necessary in order to get them to fit in those cramped wooden boxes. Some of the receptacles were not even worth of the title 'coffin,' being little more than packing crates that were far too small to accommodate the remains of a fully-grown adult.

It was nothing that a little jamming and cramming couldn't fix. The workmen stuffed a hodge-podge of various bones into each crate, often belonging to several different bodies. One man's skull might find itself packed in with a woman's rib cage and a child's limbs, to which a smattering of dirt was added in order to fill the box out and add a little weight.

When the bodies were first unearthed, they would have been in various states of decomposition. Some were little more than skeletons, dried out and desicated, but others had not entirely liquefied yet, nor had they sloughed off the remnants of their flesh and connective tissue. Even the most hard-bitten of gravediggers would feel his stomach turn at the sight of some of those corpses, finding himself suddenly overcome with a rush of queasiness on breaking open a coffin lid and catching sight of the body that lay inside.

The grisly task attracted more than its fair of ghoulish onlookers, most of them Denver residents who were attempting to satiate their morbid curiosity by catching a glimpse of some body part or other. No matter how often the workers tried to shoo them away, they always seemed to come back, sometimes in the dead of night when the workmen were long gone for the day.

Small wonder then, that ghost stories began to arise, all of them centered upon the soon-to-be-defunct graveyard. There were tales of spectral figures said to be seen wandering from grave to grave, perhaps the restless phantoms of those poor souls whose eternal rest was being disturbed by the incessant digging. Most locals then began to avoid the cemetery like the plague, fearful of its new-found reputation for being haunted. Those were superstitious times, though hardly less so than our own, and many reasoned that it surely wasn't wise to meddle in such otherworldly matters.

Despite the increasing grumblings in the press about the shoddy workmanship and the fundamental lack of respect being shown to the human remains by his employees, McGovern managed to charge the people of Denver a not-inconsiderable sum of money before public opinion finally turned fully against him.

McGovern was duly fired, but that left the city with quite the problem: what was estimated to be somewhere between 2,000 to 3,000 sets of human remains still lay buried in their original graves, undisturbed and unmoved. Many of them didn't have headstones to begin with, or any other kind of marker for that matter, either because their families were too poor to pay for one, or because there was simply nobody in their lives who cared for them enough to do so.

Rather than hire a new contractor, the city's solution to this logistical nightmare is still hard to believe – after giving the next of kin just 90 days to relocate the remains of their deceased family members to another cemetery, those bodies that were unclaimed were simply left there, abandoned and forgotten, while a new park was installed just six feet above them.

The headstones were moved, but many of the graves were left behind.

So, I believe, were the ghosts.

CHAPTER TWO

"...many coffins have not been moved..."

By 1907, fresh grass had been planted over the top of the old cemetery, and where once mourners had come to pay respects to their loved ones, now there were picnickers, spreading blankets and enjoying sunny days in Denver's brand new Cheesman Park. It had been named after Walter Cheesman, a property magnate and all-around high flyer in Denver's social circles.

Mount Calvary, the Catholic cemetery, was pretty much ignored by the Catholic church and abandoned until the 1950s and 1960s, when the botanic gardens began to take shape there.

The lion's share of ghost stories I had been told came from the Waring House, and I suspected that much of my investigation would be spent there. It is a beautiful old house, built in 1926 and gifted to the botanic gardens thirty-three years later by Dr. James Waring and his wife, Ruth. The Waring House, as it is now known, has served the Gardens in one capacity or another since 1959.

Digging into the history of the Gardens — pun very much intended — was both enlightening and saddening. The thought of so many sets of human remains buried without headstones, or even the most rudimentary of markers, was difficult to shake. So many lives that will always be unremembered. It would hardly be surprising if some of them were still haunting the site today.

In addition to the many tales of ghostly experiences and other paranormal activity, building a house on top of a former graveyard can also have other, more conventional ramifications.

Evidence of structural instability had first been noticed by the staff in 1973, with cracks appearing in the walls and floors. When a professional survey was conducted of the Waring House foundations, what the engineers found was grisly but not exactly unexpected.

The first thing that the surveyors did was to review the building's architectural history. Construction on the house had been completed in 1923. When the architects looked back with a skilled, professional eye, they found that the building's foundations had begun to shift almost immediately after it first became occupied. The worst cracking occurred in the vicinity of the library, lobby, and the drawing room; the damage was bad enough that in 1926, the sum of $20,000 – a lot of money back then – was spent in order to shore up the floor in those three areas. All of those floors were reinforced with heavy steel beams and pillars in an attempt to add stability to the sagging foundations. A crawl space was also excavated beneath the house, which would allow the foundation to be inspected periodically.

Although the Waring House continued to experience a small amount of structural movement and the warping that went along with it, the damage was relatively inconsequential for the next fifty years. Things kicked into high gear in the early 1970s, which led to the visible cracks forming and the subsequent survey.

The most significant damage was to the flagstone patio on the building's east side, where the ground had sunk at least twelve inches below its original level. Big jagged cracks were splitting the brickwork around the porch itself, threatening to bring it down.

In the vicinity of the drawing room, a three-foot deep pit had opened up outside. On the southwest corner another sixteen-inch depression was found. No wonder the staff of the botanic gardens were alarmed.

Just how stable was the ground beneath their feet?

On August 21, 1973 – coincidentally the same day that I was being born in a hospital on the opposite side of the Atlantic – a group of men congregated at the Waring House. One was the director of the botanic gardens; another was a structural engineer, highly experienced in the assessment of buildings; the third was a water engineer, a man who was well-versed in the ways in which water and soil affected structural foundations. Their goal was a straightforward one, though by no means simple: to go over the Waring house with a fine toothcomb and determine the extent of the damage it had suffered over the past half-century.

The engineers focused their efforts on the foundations of the house, making their way down into the crawlspace beneath it. Their investigation would last for several days, during which time they drilled deep down into the ground in three different spots, each one specifically chosen because it was a site of definite subsidence. In addition to drilling, the engineers also dug carefully around the building's foundation, trying to figure out why exactly the Waring House was shifting on its base.

Unfortunately, the engineers were unable to ascertain the exact cause of the house slowly sinking into the ground. They agreed that more test holes must be drilled, which duly happened two days later. Down inside the crawlspace, they dug a pair of test pits from which they took soil samples, which were sent to a lab for detailed analysis.

The results were intriguing, to say the least. Much of the soil turned out to be fill rather than natural earth, meaning that it had almost certainly been disturbed and moved there from somewhere else – something which often happens when a grave is dug and then filled in again once the casket has been lowered into it.

One of the samples contained eight feet of earth fill; another contained three feet of it, and another five feet. The Waring House was sitting on top of a great deal of disturbed earth.

At seventeen feet down, one of the drilled samples was found to contain elements of redwood, which turned out to be fragmented pieces of a coffin. Test hole number 7 contained a lot of fill material that was very clean in nature, almost indistinguishable from the natural earth that surrounded it…but thirteen feet down into the sample drill hole, more redwood pieces were found, which meant that the drill bit had pushed its way through the lid of another coffin. Four feet of void followed – about the height of a burial casket – before more pieces of wood were encountered. This was almost certainly the bottom of the same coffin. The analysis report neglected to state whether portions of human remains were encountered anywhere inside the four-foot void space in which the body would have lain.

This indicates very clearly that the area was used as a burial ground, the official report stated, and after the disintegration of the coffins, the upper soils subsided and created the settlement condition.

In other words, the Waring House was built on top of numerous coffins which, when they imploded, had disturbed the soil and caused the house to sink.

The engineers now had their consensus:

It is our opinion that the ground subsidence is essentially caused by the decomposition and collapsing of the coffins in this area. We understand the general area has been used as a cemetery during the mid to late 1800s. Since then, the cemetery has been moved from this location to Fairmount Cemetery. ***It is very possible that many coffins have not been moved*** *[author's emphasis]. It is almost certain that in the vicinity of Test Hole 1 where the front porch has failed, there are coffins in this area. We have already proved that coffins existed* *in the vicinity of Test Hole 7, and judging from the upper fill characteristics, the sunken area in the vicinity of Test Holes 8 and 9 indicates the presence of coffins.*

They also offered an explanation for why the house began to sink so rapidly over a relatively short amount of time. Due to the very nature of being a botanic garden, regular watering is necessary for the acres of plants on display.

This irrigation, while absolutely vital, had the unwanted side effect of adding a lot of water to soil that was already less than stable.

It is easy to forget that water is heavy: ask any firefighter about the reasons why buildings collapse during fire suppression operations, and they'll tell you that water weight is a definite factor. The more gallons of water that are used to extinguish a fire, the more strain is placed on the structure.

The lawns and plant life surrounding the Waring House have many more plants than the average home garden. The displays are denser and more elaborate. This has had the long-term effect of loosening the soil, and therefore weakening it. Much of this soil sat on top of the slowly decomposing coffins. While it was relatively intact, the coffins were able to maintain a certain degree of structural cohesion thanks to the soil acting like an overhead 'bridge' of sorts. Once the regular schedule of irrigation water managed to break that bridge down, the bridge collapsed and the coffins lost their shelter, which is why they collapsed and caused the ground above them to sink. This caused the foundations of the house to shift and cracks to form in the walls and floors.

In 1981, there were further concerns about the stability of the Waring House. Employees had noticed more cracks developing in the walls and depressed areas in the floor. Was it possible that one day, the structure might collapse entirely?

The only way to find out was to engage a team of experts, and so the director of Denver Botanic Gardens commissioned a report from the respected architectural firm of Long-Hoeft. More testing was done, and the news was not good: the subsidence was getting worse, and showed no signs of stopping or even slowing down.

While also referring to the 1973 report, this new report ended on a distinctly ominous note:

In addition to the probability of coffin collapse, there is another explicit problem given in the core analysis. The building is constructed in an area of significant fill; eight of the eleven cores [sample holes] report fill material. Much of the fill most probably is burial backfill, but not all of it. The fill varied from three feet in depth in hole five and six to almost sixteen feet in hole 1. Regardless of its origin, the existence [sic] of this amount of fill under a building is worrisome.

There is no reason to believe that the fill received proper compaction to enable equal bearing capacities from one fill to another, or to enable bearing capacities equivalent to undisturbed soil. ***With time, and with moisture, settling will occur*** [author's emphasis].

As time passes, irrigation continues. The Waring House stands on relatively unsteady ground to this day, and with every passing week the level of incremental subsidence grows worse. Nobody is entirely sure how many coffins still lie undiscovered beneath the building, each one ready to collapse when the time – and pressure – is right.

When one walks through the ground floor of the Waring House today, not to mention the grounds of the botanic gardens which surround it, they would do well to tread lightly. Not too far beneath their feet lie the coffins and bodies of Denver's nineteenth century dead, and their spirits might not wish to be disturbed.

My team of paranormal investigators and I would have five nights locked in with them to try and figure that out for ourselves.

As things turned out, they were not going to disappoint us.

CHAPTER THREE
Ghosts in the Gardens

Before starting off the investigation, I had the opportunity to interview a couple of witnesses to the strange goings-on at the botanic gardens.

The first was Paula Vanderbilt, a paranormal enthusiast who has visited Cheesman Park and the area around Denver Botanic Gardens on several occasions, drawn by the many ghost stories that surround the place. When she heard that I was researching the haunting and writing a book on the subject, she graciously agreed to talk about her experiences there.

"On one of my visits there, I took an Ovilus with me," she explained during our interview. "The Ovilus said my name at least three times, which I found very impressive."

The Ovilus is a controversial device among paranormal investigators, having both its supporters and its detractors, most of whom hold very strong opinions about the device.

The Ovilus is said to work by associating words in an electronic database with energy levels in the surrounding environment. The theory goes that spirit entities are somehow able to manipulate those energy levels in order to spell out meaningful words and phrases.

In this author's experience, much of the time the Ovilus spits out a stream of meaningless gibberish...but on more than one occasion, I have seen it be almost scarily accurate. As it turned out, the device would come up with some very interesting things during our investigation of the Gardens.

One example of a fascinating Ovilus hit took place during an investigation at the Grant-Humphreys Manson, another of Denver's historic haunted properties. Two of my colleagues were employing an Ovilus without any results. When I walked over to join them, the box immediately said the word *'paramedic'* – which happens to be my chosen profession. The Ovilus had never used that word before, despite having been run for multiple sessions, and all three of us were duly impressed by how specific a hit it seemed to have made. Some will dismiss the idea by pointing out that even a broken clock will tell the correct time twice a day, but I have found the Ovilus to be a very effective tool on certain occasions. The chances of the name *Paula,* for example, randomly coming up three times during the same session aren't all that high, statistically speaking, but that is exactly what happened when Paula visited the botanic gardens.

As she walked around Cheesman Park with her friend

Rhonda and a few like-minded acquaintances, the Ovilus continued to pipe up with new words. Something that really got her attention was the phrase 'wear the jewelry,' the three words all coming in rapid succession. This took her aback because she happened to be wearing some jewelry that day which had been left to her by her grandmother.

Once again, we have to ask whether this was attributable to mere coincidence, or if it could have been a genuine communication with some kind of spirit entity. Paula strongly believes that it was the latter.

Impressed, the ladies wandered past the back side of the Pavilion. Rhonda suddenly spotted a dog running across the road. Concerned for its safety, she called out, but when the runaway pooch reached the center of the street, it disappeared into thin air right before her astonished eyes.

The dog wasn't hit by a car or obscured from view by passing traffic, she insists; it quite literally was there one instant and gone the next. The dog was large in size and its coat was light, like that of a Golden Retriever or Labrador. Rhonda had seen it very clearly and could describe it in great detail.

Paula has taken the 'Ghosts in the Gardens' tour twice. During her first visit, which began in the Boettcher

Conservatory, the entire tour group heard the sound of a piano playing from somewhere within the building – except that there was no piano to be played. The music faded away.

Standing in the lobby and listening to their tour guide, Paula noticed that her friend Jessica appeared to be a little nervous. In a whisper, she asked Jessica what was wrong.

"Somebody just tapped me on the shoulder," she replied, looking warily over her shoulder. Nobody was standing behind her...or at least, nobody that could be seen.

The shoulder–tapping seems to be a fairly common phenomenon at the Gardens, as several visitors that I have spoken to reported it. This seems to be a playful occurrence, and certainly nothing to worry about.

As the tour continued, the music returned. The tour guide seemed perplexed, unable to explain where it might be coming from. The group made its way up the street to the Waring House. As they were entering through the lobby, one of the female guests let out a yelp. This startled the entire group, who all turned to look at the woman. She was clutching her arm and said that she had just felt something scratch her.

Sure enough, when the tour guide checked the guest's arm underneath the main lights, an angry red scratch was seen running across the surface of her skin from lower forearm to wrist. Her demeanor changed on the spot from that of the curious visitor to a state of concerned hyper-awareness, looking into every corner and pool of shadow in case something was hiding there.

The tour group took seats in the Great Room. The guests were all good spirits, yet their laughter had a slightly nervous edge to it after the curious scratching incident had taken place. Most could not help but wonder where this was a simple case of self-inflicted attention-seeking or something a little more sinister: an entity that wanted to make its presence felt in the clearest terms imaginable.

After the group had taken a short break, their guide led them out of the Waring House once more and into the darkness. They made their way around the perimeter, listening to some of the spookier stories that visitors and staff members had experienced among the flora and fauna of the botanic gardens. Paula continued to listen, but also kept a wary eye out for anything unusual. It was a chilly night, and she was glad that she had wrapped up in warm clothes before venturing outside.

What the tour guide said next made her blood run cold. Gesturing in the direction of Cheesman Park, he explained that one of the more common ghost sightings from that particular area was the apparition of a dog that ran out into the road and then suddenly vanished into thin air…

With a casual, offhand comment, the guide seemed to have validated Rhonda's earlier ghost sighting. He was indicating the area behind the Pavilion, which was the same place they had been standing on that earlier visit.

When she asked for more details about the dog, the guide described it as being large with a light-colored coat. The conclusion seemed inescapable: her friend Rhonda had been just one of several people to have witnessed the same apparition in the same location.

Nor was this the only paranormal experience she reported at the botanic gardens. During a public tour of the Waring House the year before, both Paula and her boyfriend had been standing in the area of the kitchen looking out of the window, when both of them caught side of a shadow figure running along the edge of the wall outside. They both looked at one another in astonishment, wanting to know if the other one had seen what they had seen.

Comparing notes afterward, Paula and her boyfriend agreed that the shadow figure had been about the height of a small child. Could this possibly have been the ghost of the young boy that many have claimed haunts the Waring House?

They checked carefully to make sure that there were no children on the tour (there weren't) and then went on to confirm that no kids were wandering around in the grounds outside, playing.

Strange events such as those experienced by Paula are not all that uncommon at the botanic gardens. Every year, visitors share stories of their weird encounters. While such phenomena have been documented all around the botanic gardens and across Cheesman park too, it seems that the majority of them center upon the Waring House.

The story told to me by the next lady I interviewed also took place there, and I began to wonder just exactly what it was about the Waring House that made it such a hot spot for paranormal activity.

Each year, as the month of October draws near, and Halloween approaches, the thoughts of most people will inevitably turn toward the subject of ghosts. Ask any paranormal investigator and they will freely tell you that they receive more calls for help and more requests from the media to perform interviews in October than at any other time of the year.

For the staff of Denver Botanic Gardens, it is no different. They relish putting on their 'Ghosts in the Gardens' tours. Led by an experienced and expert guide, visitors are escorted on a guided tour of the Gardens. The reader may recall that it was after taking this same tour that my boss's sister-in-law felt compelled to relate some of the spooky stories to him, which led to him suggesting that I conduct an investigation there.

Back in 2012, Rose Glenn took the Ghosts in the Gardens tour. Of all the various stops along the way, the location that intrigued her the most was the Waring House. Wandering around the grand old house, Rose began taking pictures all over the place, photographing whatever caught her eye. As a paranormal enthusiast, this wasn't her first rodeo – she was used to spending time in haunted places, and experience had taught her to take as many photos as she possibly could. After all, one never knew what might decide to show itself…

Rose also used an infrared camera (IR) rather than the standard model that most people are used to. There is a prominent theory among members of the paranormal research community that because IR cameras are able to 'see' more of the spectrum than just visible light, they may also be capable of capturing the images of spirit entities. A number of intriguing photographs exist that lend credence to this theory, and many paranormal investigators and enthusiasts use both regular and IR cameras, alternating between the two.

One of the characteristics of an IR camera is that it lends the photographs taken with it a distinctly pink-purple hue. She saw nothing out of the ordinary as she walked slowly from room to room inside the Waring House. It was only afterward, when she downloaded the digital photographs to her computer and looked through them on the monitor screen, that she noticed something odd.

Rose had been standing in the front lobby, close to the main doorway, when she snapped the picture. She was framing the main staircase carefully. Rose is one hundred percent certain that nobody else was standing either on or around the staircase when she took the photograph, and yet when one scrutinizes the image carefully it is possible to see what looks like the figure of a young child staring straight back into the camera.

There are a number of ghost stories in circulation

concerning the spirit of a young boy who is believed by some to haunt the Waring House, but Rose thinks that the figure in her photograph is that of a little girl in a dress. Both Rose and some of the people that she has shown the picture to have said that they can see a second human-shaped figure, this one mistier and lacking in substance, standing partway up the staircase behind that of the little girl.

It is interesting to note that according to staff at the Gardens, a coffin was unearthed in the gardens several years ago, containing the remains of a little girl wearing a frilly, old-fashioned dress.

Like any good investigator who is unwillingly to simply take the picture at face value, Rose attempted to debunk her own work. She recalled there being a tapestry hanging on the wall of the staircase, which she subsequently confirmed by looking back through the rest of her photographs. Was it possible, she wondered, that her eyes were playing tricks on her, misinterpreting the intricate swirls and arcs of the embroidery for a child's face? This is a very real phenomenon which goes by the name of pareidolia: the human brain is innately wired to want to see the human face or form in random patterns. Many paranormal enthusiasts refer to this same condition as 'matrixing.' Perhaps the example we are all most familiar with is that of the Man in the Moon, composed of the long-dead lunar seas and plateaus. Even though we know that there is no true face there, our eye is nonetheless all too willing to be fooled.

In an attempt to answer this perplexing question, Rose went back and took photographs of the staircase from multiple angles, including the same vantage point from which she had taken the original picture, giving particular emphasis to the hanging tapestry. No matter how many times she tried, she was unable to replicate the effect. Neither the child, the misty figure, or anything remotely like either of them appeared on any of the other pictures. At the time of writing, the mystery of what exactly they are remains unsolved.

Fascinated with Denver Botanic Gardens in general and the Waring House in particular, Rose returned for another tour three years later. During her October 2015 visit, she took a picture on the balcony at the top of the stairs, with the camera pointing in the direction of the administrative offices. Once again, Rose hadn't seen anything out of place when she took the photo, but another mysterious figure appeared when she blew it up on her computer screen.

It must be said that taking photographs of mirrors, glass,

or any other reflective surface can often be a double-edged sword. On the one hand, the use of mirrors in order to make some kind of contact with the dead has a long historical precedent – the procedure is known as scrying, and goes all the way back to ancient times. It is a technique that this author has employed several times with varying degrees of success.

On the other hand, we return once again to the thorny subject of pareidolia. When the light falls on a reflective surface such as a mirror or the surface of a window in a certain way, it can form a pattern that is very reminiscent of a face or a figure. That's why most paranormal investigators are very wary of ghostly images that turn up in windows and mirrors; although there are a number of impressive seemingly anomalous photos taken in this way, in many cases it is impossible to tell the difference between the paranormal and pareidolia.

With that being said, Rose's photograph is intriguing. Her focus was the window of an empty office. She had allowed the rest of the tour to go on ahead of her, affording her a little privacy. Once the last person had reached the bottom of the staircase and disappeared from sight, she began taking a battery of pictures, one of which was the image in question.

This time she was using an iPhone rather than the IR camera, which meant that the image resolution wasn't quite as sharp as it might have been. Nevertheless, when one looks at the photograph and concentrates on the office window, a human-shaped figure is plainly visible. Rose believes that it is the figure of a nurse or a perhaps a nun, which is no great stretch, she points out, given the proximity of the Waring House to the old Catholic burial ground and the nearby 'pest house' for those with serious diseases and illnesses.

After looking at the picture, I cannot help but agree with her. The figure does appear to be wearing a black wimple (the head-dress commonly worn by nuns) that is edged in white. It also looks to my eye as though the figure might be carrying a baby or a small child clutched to her chest.

The photograph is remarkable, and once again, neither Rose or I can offer an explanation for how the figure or figures manifested on it. They would have to have been standing inside one of the closed and locked offices at the time she took the photograph, and had they been flesh and blood people then she would surely have noticed them through the glass.

Inexplicable photos aren't the only strange thing that

Rose has experienced at the Waring House, and she cheerfully reports that the historic old building 'never disappoints!' On one occasion she took an Ovilus in with her. The device instantly began spitting out words that seemed very meaningful, with the word BURIED being particularly common. TRAPPED and HELP weren't far behind, and she wonders if this was an attempt by the spirits of the dead whose bodies still lie beneath the Waring House to communicate with its living occupants.

On another visit, Rose felt herself tapped lightly on the shoulder by something unseen — an experience that numerous others have experienced, including (though I did not yet know it at the time of our interview) the author of this book. When Rose whirled around to see who was trying to get her attention, she found that there was nobody there. She also heard distinct knocking sounds coming from one of the rooms behind her. When she went to check on who was making the noise, she found that the room was completely empty.

It seems that if one happens to be in the right place at the right time, the phantom residents of the Waring House are still only too willing to make their presence known. My team and I were to learn this lesson for ourselves during our five nights of investigation there.

Having talked to Rose and listened to her experiences, I was more enthusiastic than ever to find out whether the spirits of the botanic gardens were willing to come out and interact with us.

It was high time we went to go and meet them.

CHAPTER FOUR

"I Have Never Been More Terrified in My Life."

In an article titled *Haunted Ghost Cemetery Under Botanic Gardens Spooks Visitors* by Jean Lotus *(https://patch.com/colorado/denver/haunted-denver-ghost-cemetery-under-botanic-gardens-spooks-visitors)* Botanic Gardens Director of Education Matt Cole listed a litany of strange events that had been reported by visiting members of the public.

Unexplained mists, the smell of cigar smoke, and one visitor getting their pant leg pulled by something invisible while touring the dining room of the Waring House, were just three examples.

Another visitor heard the sound of a woman sighing, while another found their phone going haywire, shooting a burst of eighteen pictures without them ever touching the button. A third smelled lilacs (which weren't in bloom at the time) and had their ear flicked, presumably by something unseen.

Over at the Rocky Mountain Paranormal Research Society website, *(https://www.rockymountainparanormal.com/cheesmanstory*

.html) somebody purporting to be a security guard at the botanic gardens told their own story. In addition to seeing smoky human-shaped figures and full-bodied apparitions, this person claimed to have heard a wealth of auditory phenomena, such as the sound of a woman screaming, hearing his own name whispered into his ear, slamming doors, and disembodied footsteps.

Physical phenomena were also reported, including numerous incidences of people being touched by something that they could not see. I sat up and really paid attention when the writer claimed that they had video footage of a young boy, who was seen peeking around the edge of a filing cabinet on the hidden back staircase of the Waring House. Stories of a young boy haunting the Waring House had reached me from several sources, and I found myself wondering whether this ghostly young man would make his presence known to us when we began spending the night there.

Now that my team and I were well-versed in the history of the old cemetery and the botanic gardens themselves, the next step was for us to actually put boots on the ground and get to grips with the location for real.

Although I'm a big fan of the lockdown method, which involves the investigators being sealed inside the building for many hours or days at a time, we decided to save that for the second night and for those that came after it. I wanted night one to be a relatively low-key affair, with the goal of getting everybody acquainted with the particulars of the case and conducting an interview or two.

The background research that I had done strongly suggested that much of the haunting was centered around the Waring House, which was home to much of the administrative staff and their offices. I intended to spend the lion's share of the investigation trying to unravel its mysteries.

Before that, however, I intended to speak with an employee named Emily. The word was that she was a firm believer in the botanic gardens being haunted, and was willing to consent to being interviewed.

At the time of our interview, Emily Kline was working as a Facility Custodial Technician at the botanic gardens. Her duties include setting up and tearing down the items needed for the many weddings and other special events that take place there all year round.

When we sat down together in the spacious lobby of the Gardens for an interview, she had worked there for a little under one year. Even in that relatively short space of time, Emily had experienced her own encounters with the paranormal.

The events of her most memorable story took place in the Morrison Discovery Center, one of the Gardens' smaller structures. The building consists of the Children's Education offices, bathrooms, a storage closet, and a small greenhouse. When Emily first began working at the Gardens, another employee told her that she often heard strange sounds coming from somewhere within the building when she worked there. Finding the idea to be just a little too far-fetched for her liking, Emily brushed it off with a polite nod and a smile.

When the employee in question moved on to another job, Emily assumed a new set of responsibilities, which meant that she spent more time working in the Morrison building.

Early one morning, Emily was involved in the unglamorous but necessary task of cleaning the bathrooms. When she heard the sound of footsteps coming from the room next door, she quite reasonably assumed that another employee was approaching. As she listened for a little while longer, however, she soon realized that there was something rather odd about these particular footsteps – they sounded as if they were dragging along the ground. The cadence of the steps was slow, almost lazy, which didn't really fit with the mannerisms of any of Emily's colleagues.

Looking around, Emily didn't see anybody that might be responsible for the footsteps. Trying to find a rational explanation for something that seemed more than a little odd, she thought that maybe the sounds weren't actually footsteps at all. Perhaps they were the noises made by the ducts as air rushed through them, or something of that nature This was proven false just a moment later when the vents ceased flowing air, and still the footsteps continued.

They were now getting louder and moving closer toward her.

Starting to feel just a little uncomfortable, Emily got up and left the building without looking back.

"Morrison is so small that there is absolutely no way somebody could have been in there and hidden from sight," she explained. "The footsteps were coming from inside a building that was completely empty, except for me."

Suddenly her former colleague's stories didn't seem quite so far-fetched.

As mentioned earlier, much of the ghostly activity at the Gardens seems to take place at the Waring House. "It's a nice house," Emily agreed when I broached the subject with her, "but it's really eerie. Even before I had heard some of the stories surrounding the house, I used to walk in there and get a really bad, almost oppressive feeling about ninety percent of the time."

This echoed the sentiments of one of the night security guards I interviewed. He was a very level-headed and matter-of-fact man who nonetheless admitted that he didn't like looking up at the windows of the Waring House when he made his rounds in the wee small hours.

One evening, she accompanied a security guard named Mike across to the Waring House and waited for him while he finished his final checks of the day. He went about the methodical business of closing the house for the night and locking it up, as he had done countless times before. With nothing better to do while she waited, Emily made a snap decision to try an impromptu EVP recording session right then and there. Perhaps, she reasoned, the spirits of the Waring House would have something to say to her.

While Mike headed to the front of the house, keys in hand, she sat down on a chair in the entrance hall, took out her cell phone and began to record an audio voice memo.

The house was quiet, save for the gentle ticking of the clock which stands at the foot of the main staircase. She and Mike were the only two living people in the building.

"Is there anybody there?" Emily asked hesitantly, feeling just a little silly for talking into thin air. After all, this was how practically every Hollywood movie séance started out.

In apparent response, odd noises started coming from somewhere upstairs. A chill went through her. As best she could tell, these weren't footsteps. It sounded as if a number of objects were being moved around up there. The noises went on for just a few seconds and then abruptly ceased as quickly as they had started.

Playing Devil's Advocate, I asked whether this could simply have been the building settling down. Most structures tend to expand during the day when the weather is warm and contract at night when they cool down, which can lead to all manner of creaks and groans. Emily is convinced that this wasn't what she heard at the Waring House that night. For one thing, the sounds came in rapid succession, one after the other, and seemed to come as a direct response to her questions whenever she asked them.

When Mike came back in a few minutes later, he found a distinctly jittery Emily waiting for him. Asking him whether he had gone upstairs and moved anything around, he flatly denied having done so. Whatever it was that had caused the sounds, it certainly hadn't been him. Nor had he heard anything amiss while he made his rounds.

"Let's go and check it out," he said after listening to her story, leading a distinctly reluctant Emily upstairs. Together, the pair searched the upper floor of the house, including the offices which were always kept locked in order to provide an additional level of security.

Needless to say, they found nothing out of place.

"Have you had any strange experiences in THIS building?" I asked, gesturing to the lobby all around us where my fellow paranormal investigators were setting up recording equipment in preparation for the night ahead. It turned out that something odd had indeed happened in the same lobby only the week before.

Emily had been sweeping the floor in front of the doors to Mitchell Hall. "Despite hearing all of the ghost stories, nothing has ever really frightened me while I have been working here," she began. Then, looking me right in the eye, she said, "I've got to tell you that I have never been more terrified in my life…"

Fascinated, I asked Emily if she knew why she felt that way. She shook her head, telling me that the feeling came over her all of a sudden, without any apparent cause. When asked to put it into words, she described it as "a really dark, ominous feeling that made me feel like I should leave because something really didn't want me here."

Trying her best to shrug the feeling off, Emily went back to work with the broom. She reached the far end of the lobby, set down the dustpan, and looked up from her work just as a loud bang came from one of the doors. Blinking in surprise, Emily was amazed to see that the door was moving in its frame, as though somebody had hit or kicked it forcefully from the opposite side.

The door in question led to the Boettcher Memorial Tropical Conservatory, or, as I couldn't help but think of it after being given a tour of the place, 'Jurassic Park.' The conservatory was a sea of green flora and fauna, covered from floor to ceiling in lush plants and trees that seemed as if they would be more at home in a jungle or tropical rain forest than in a building in the heart of Denver. Such is the magic of a botanic garden, however, a 14-acre oasis of plant life set among Denver's 155 square miles of concrete, steel, and asphalt.

The conservatory is named after Claude K. Boettcher, once known to all and sundry as 'the wealthiest man in the West,' and his wife Edna. Not content with simply being a titan of the Colorado business world (not to mention the Boettchers being extremely prominent on the Denver social scene) Claude was renowned for his deep sense of philanthropy. He established the Boettcher Foundation in 1937, with the express intent of bettering the lives of his fellow Coloradans, particularly those who had been dealt a bad hand in life. The Foundation poured money into several regional hospitals, and established a dedicated school for physically handicapped children.

When he passed away in 1957, a vast sum of money was left to his Foundation, which still continues to offer scholarships and supports other charitable endeavors to this day.

On an interesting side note, the mansion that Claude and his wife Edna purchased in 1924 was built by the Cheesman family and sold to the Boettchers by Mr. Cheesman's widow after his death. It too was left to the Boettcher Foundation after the passing of Claude and Edna, who died the year after her husband. The Foundation in turn gifted it to the State of Colorado, which set it aside as a permanent residence for the Governor of Colorado. Governor Bill Owens issued an executive order in January of 2003 that designated the house "The Governor's Residence at the Boettcher Mansion." The mansion still stands today at 400 East 8th Avenue, and is well worth a visit (at the time of writing, tours are given free of charge).

A generous $600,000 grant from the Foundation was bestowed upon Denver Botanic Gardens in 1963 so that a conservatory could be built to house exotic plants from around the world. Standing outside the Boettcher Memorial Conservatory, one is struck by its truly unique and bold architectural design. There is a somewhat science fiction-esque quality to the structure, with its soaring concrete arches, most of which are studded with an array of angled windows. It bears a strong similarity to the many facets of a diamond, particularly when the sun glints at just the right angle from the Plexiglas windows.

Completed in 1966, the conservatory has delighted visitors from far and wide for more than fifty years. After all, where else can one find over 1,000 tropical and sub-tropical plants under the same roof?

One might find it strange to believe that such a thoroughly modern building should be haunted, but how else are we to explain what happened to Emily and Mike?

Startled by the loud bang on the door, Emily immediately called out for Mike to come back. He listened calmly to her story and then said that he would go and see for himself just who this mysterious door-thumper was. There was bound to be a perfectly rational explanation, he reasoned. Maybe a late visitor had gotten accidentally trapped inside the conservatory when the building closed down for the night.

When Mike went inside to check, he found the conservatory completely empty, with the exception of a few frogs and resident insects. Nothing stirred inside the cavernous greenhouse. Puzzled, he wrote it off as simply being one of those weird things that happened around the botanic gardens at night, and went about his rounds as usual.

The following night, Emily and Mike were working on a leaky fountain inside the lobby, trying to figure out where exactly the source of the leak was. Mike's phone rang. Telling Emily that he had to go and take care of another matter that had arisen, he left her to continue troubleshooting the fountain on her own.

Hearing a noise from the direction of the conservatory again, she looked up and saw the same door shaking and rattling against the jamb. Being made of glass, the doors would clearly show anybody who might be standing on the other side...but there was nobody there. Rather than the violent impact she had witnessed the night before, the door now seemed to be being shaken from the opposite side as though somebody was trying to open it.

"MIKE!"

Mike hurried back to join her, but by the time he arrived the door was still and silent again. Perplexed, the security guard marked the time on his watch, and then went to search the conservatory. Predictably, it was completely empty once again, just as he had expected.

Next, the two of them went to check the video files from the CCTV camera which covered the door. Mike rolled the footage back a few minutes and hit the play button.

The security camera had a good view of the door, which was well-lit from behind. Peering intently at the monitor screen, they watched in fascination as a dark shadow flitted across the gap between the door and its frame, blocking out the background light for just a second.

Someone – or something – had been moving around

inside the empty conservatory, and based upon the time stamp, it had been just seconds before Emily had seen the door being shaken. The moving shadow was quite clearly visible on the video playback, and yet Mike's search of the conservatory proved that there should have been no-one or nothing inside there capable of blocking out that light. Its origin remains a mystery.

One interesting point is that the first incident took place at 8:20pm, and the second happened three minutes after that on the following evening. Although two data points do not necessarily make a pattern, they are at least suggestive. I checked my own watch. It was just coming up to eight o'clock. I asked my fellow investigators to set up a remote camera in order to watch the door, in the hope that we would get a repeat performance.

When I asked Emily whether she had experienced anything else that was unusual while working at the botanic gardens, she told me that on several occasions she had been unaccountably overcome with strong emotions that came right out of the blue. Sometimes the feeling would be one of sadness, while at other times she would suddenly develop a strong sense of anger.

There was never an obvious cause for these feelings,

such as an argument with a co-worker or receiving bad news. The one thing that these emotions have in common is that they are always negative in nature. They are never happy, joyful, or euphoric. Emily says that she is not normally prone to such feelings in her everyday life, and has never experienced anything like it outside of the botanic gardens.

My team and I sat and watched the door to the Boettcher Memorial Conservatory for over an hour, recording it with several video cameras. Unfortunately, the mysterious door rattler failed to put in an appearance for us. Perhaps whoever or whatever it was, was simply feeling camera-shy.

It may be that the conditions just weren't right for it to manifest. One of the most frustrating ways for paranormal investigators to spend their time is in waiting for lightning to strike twice in the same place, but sometimes it actually DOES happen. More often than not, however, it turns out to be fruitless. Such was the case when my colleagues and I staked out the place where Emily had had her bizarre experience.

Fortunately for us, the botanic gardens would turn out to have many other surprises in store.

CHAPTER FIVE
Get Me Out of Here

I was just wrapping up my interview with Emily Kline when another employee walked over and asked to speak to me. Rose Garcia is a temporary cleaner at Denver Botanic Gardens, and as such knows practically every nook and cranny...after all, her job is to keep them all neat and tidy.

She had just happened to overhear our conversation, and wanted to tell me about something that had happened to her earlier in the week.

Rose said that she had been cleaning a rest room on the west side of the building, humming a tune and minding her own business, when she had suddenly heard a girl's voice call out the words, "Get me out of here."

The voice seemed to have originated from the ladies' locker room next door.

When Rose went in to check, there was of course nobody to be found. Seconds later, Rose heard the exact same words repeated once again. She described the girl's voice as sounding 'real light,' but the words were extremely clear and easy to make out.

I asked whether the girl's tone of voice had sounded

upset or frightened, which would seem quite likely given the words she had chosen, but Rose shook her head. No, she explained, the girl had sounded very calm and matter-of-fact, and hadn't seemed to be particularly distressed about anything.

When I enquired about the possibility of there being somebody back there – perhaps another employee who was working very late that night, for example – she told me that it was extremely unlikely.

"I'll take you back there if you like, let you have a look around," she offered, leading the way toward the ladies' locker room.

"I'm going to hide behind you," I said, earning myself a laugh. There weren't too many potential hiding places, and while the idea of a prankster on the staff being responsible wasn't beyond the realm of possibility, every employee that I spoke to told me the same thing: workers at the botanic gardens didn't play tricks on one another like that. There were more than enough genuinely weird things going on, so what was the point in faking it?

"I've heard some crazy stories around here," she said, shaking her head. "I just try to mind my own business and get on with my work. I don't bother them and they don't bother me."

"That's a very smart approach to take," I agreed. In my experience (and that of most of my peers in this field) the more somebody takes an interest in the paranormal, the more it tends to take an interest in them right back. Sometimes it really can be best to just leave this stuff alone, unless you have some taken some serious preventative measure (by which I mean spiritual protection) or are willing to accept the consequences…consequences that can sometimes be very negative and disturbing.

It pays to be on your guard sometimes.

We spent the remainder of the evening conducting a number of experiments in the vicinity of Boettcher. Sadly, none of them yielded anything in the way of results. No EVPs, unusual electromagnetic or temperature readings, not even a light anomaly was found.

It is a fairly common custom among paranormal researchers that once four o'clock in the morning comes around and nothing much seems to be happening, despite the very best efforts of the investigators to stimulate something, then they are pretty much done for the night. After talking amongst ourselves, that was the conclusion we unanimously arrived at.

It didn't necessarily mean that this particular part of the Gardens wasn't haunted — it was far too early to tell — but based on our distinct lack of results so far, it didn't seem like a prudent place to devote a great deal more of our time or effort.

I could only hope that during the next few nights of our investigation, which was scheduled to take place at the Waring House, the hunting would be better.

For our second night of investigation, we relocated from the Boettcher Memorial Conservatory over to the Waring House. I took a slightly larger team this time. In addition to myself, there was also Seth, Stan, Linda, and Jen. Three of them were seasoned investigators, whereas Jen was relatively new to the field and still learning some of the ins and outs of field work.

A massage therapist by profession, Seth had been with my team since its earliest days. He was a very calm and laid-back type of guy, one who could always be depended upon to bring a sense of equilibrium to an investigation. I couldn't recall ever having seen him get worked up or angry, let alone nervous during a case. Seth also possessed a whimsical sense of humor, and wasn't afraid to show it, but when it came time to investigate, he was always one hundred percent professional.

Stan made his living detailing cars. He had applied to join BCPRS after attending a lecture that we had given at a local library. His interest in the paranormal had led him to apply with us for an investigator's position.

I had first met Jen at the private ambulance company where we had both worked. As the Clinical Chief, Jen was my boss (I was the Assistant Clinical Chief, she was the chief) and we both worked well together. I liked and respected her tremendously. She had always expressed an interest in the field of paranormal research, listening to the stories and experiences I brought back from each investigation, and finally she took the plunge and applied to join us as a probationary investigator. Having another paramedic on the team was a definite asset, and she always kept her cool in a crisis.

I know people who have spent less money on buying their home and car than Linda has spent on ghost hunting. This medical professional had always been fascinated with the paranormal, and never missed an opportunity to get out into the field and investigate an allegedly haunted location. Along with her husband, Jason, Linda had amassed enough high-tech gadgetry to equip an entire branch of Radio Shack. She also had the knowledge and savvy to know how to use every single piece of that equipment. Linda and Jason had accompanied me on a journey across the Atlantic to England, where we investigated the infamous 30 East Drive (known in America as 'the Black Monk House' due to its connection with the Black Monk of Pontefract) and the mysterious Woodchester Mansion, to name just two places.

We were all very excited to be spending the night inside the Waring House. Although the Boettcher Memorial Conservatory had been a fascinating place, its modernity lacked the historic charm of this grand old house. Walking up the front path, we were met by the security guard, who kindly unlocked the front door and let us inside.

The interior was impressive. We spent our first few minutes just taking in the grandeur of the place, admiring the artwork and artisanship that had been put into its construction and decor.

After a little discussion, we decided to set up shop in the Great Room. It was by far the largest open space inside the house. There were more than enough tables set out to hold our equipment cases, not to mention the enormous stash of junk food that would sustain us throughout the night. (Most paranormal investigations are fueled by caffeinated beverages of one sort or another).

Once we had laid out our gear, I gave the team a brief tour of the property, relaying some of the snippets of information that I had been given on my first visit to the Waring House. Stepping into the kitchen, I pointed out what had once been the wall-mounted electric bells that had been used to call for service from elsewhere in the house. The wires to those bells had been cut some time ago, meaning that it should have been impossible for them ever to sound again; yet the director had assured me that they had been heard ringing on more than one occasion by staff at the botanic gardens.

Finding this absolutely fascinating, we set about trying to debunk the idea that it might be paranormal. Perhaps vibrations in the walls and floor were to blame, we thought? Two minutes of a fairly sizable man jumping up and down next to them failed to make them ring, and that should have caused more than ample vibrations to take place.

What about the possibility of the wind having caused the

phenomenon – the old house may not have been particularly well-insulated, after all, so perhaps a draft or a breeze might have set the bells off? We stood around, blowing as hard as we could manage onto the bells, not caring whether we looked silly or not. The bells remained obstinately silent no matter how hard we blew on them. So much for that theory…

When all was said and done, the only method we could find of making the bells give even the slightest tinkle was to touch them directly, tapping them lightly with a fingertip. None of us were able to come up with a suitably non-paranormal explanation for the bells ringing, and yet several employees had witnessed it taking place.

Another area that fascinated us was the hidden staircase. Located behind a swinging bookcase in one of the office areas, the narrow wooden staircase was something that you wouldn't ever suspect was there unless somebody told you about it. Once again, it was the kind of thing you would expect to see on an episode of *Scooby Doo*. It turned out that if you took hold of the bottom step and lifted, an entire section of the lower staircase swung upward on hinges. The open space that was then revealed was used for storage, yet I couldn't help but wonder if it was originally used to conceal something…perhaps liquor during the Prohibition era, which was in effect until 1933?

The staircase led up to the second floor. Kevin Pharris, author of *The Haunted Heart of Denver*, theorizes that this may have been a staircase used by the servants and household staff to access an upstairs bedroom. In his book, Kevin states that "opening the stairs awakens the ghosts in the Waring House." Just in case that was true, and manipulating the staircase was a trigger for paranormal activity in the house, I made sure to open them up and leave them that way for a few minutes. (I like to cover all the bases).

While my team set out to conduct some baseline readings and start setting up a few experiments, I found a quiet corner and sat down to review some of the background material that the staff had provided me with. Whenever something that could possibly be considered paranormal took place at the botanic gardens, it was diligently written down in a notebook by those who experienced it. As I looked through the pages, the sheer variety of strange happenings was striking.

Here are just a few of those notes, written in exact words of those who experienced them.

When we arrived at the Lilac Garden, the air was quite warm. Then we heard about the little girl. When we left, it was bone-chilling cold.

A wind-chime sound in the library 2X.

I heard a faint wind-chime in the library by the book scanner.

I heard what sounded like chimes in the library. While standing outside the Waring House, I saw a black shadow go by one of the windows on the main level.

(Author's note — the reader may recall that the black shadow passing by the main level windows was *exactly* the same thing that was reported by Paula Vanderbilt and her companion).

Heard what sounded like wind chimes in the library. Out int the garden, saw what appeared to be a ball of light disappear into the bushes.

(Author's note — based on the lack of a detailed description, these *four* separate reports of wind chimes could perhaps have been ambient noise coming from outside the building. It is interesting that all of them occurred in the library. Three of them occurred on the same day, and the fourth took place on the day before. This may be explainable by the presence of wind chimes in a neighboring house, close enough to the Gardens for the sound to carry across).

In the Waring House kitchen, I was standing in front of the ice box. No-one was standing near me when I felt a hand touch my right forearm. A light touch and friendly. No-one was visible.

Outside the Carriage House, I saw a mist swirling up from the raised garden bed, like a young child turning in a dance.

Smelled a cigar.
(Author's note: there are numerous accounts of cigar smoke being smelled when nobody in the area is smoking).

I heard a girl in the Waring House dinner room. Also

what sounded like a sigh from a woman, and other noises.

I got scratched over at the house immediately when we walked in.

Walking through the kitchen of the Waring House, just before passing the basement stares, a strong compression started on my chest, right on the sternum. As soon as we left the building, it let up.

At the end of the tour in the Waring House, while our group stood in the meeting room, I saw a black figure with red eyes standing next to the mirror in the entryway.

My pant legs were being pulled repeatedly in the Waring House dining room.

As I closed the journal and set it aside, I started thinking about the diverse range of bizarre things that visitors reported having experienced. It was difficult to miss the fact that most of the human senses were involved. Visitors saw shadow figures and light anomalies. They heard the sound of a girl and that of a woman sighing. Physical sensations such as being touched lightly, clothes being tugged, and also, more ominously, one account of being scratched. Peculiar smells also seemed to abound.

This haunting was beginning to look as if it checked all the boxes, running the full gamut of paranormal phenomena.

I stood up and stretched. It was time to check on my team. Walking from room to room, I was disheartened to hear that despite their very best efforts, nothing remotely out of the ordinary seemed to be happening.

"It's far too quiet in here tonight," Jen said, giving voice to what we were all thinking. "The atmosphere just feels really flat."

She was right. It did. Even somebody as insensitive to psychic matters as I was, could tell that there was no energy in the place.

The next few hours were an exercise in frustration. No matter which technique or piece of equipment that we tried, the result was nothing. Even changing our location within the house, moving between rooms, floors, and staircases didn't help…

…until the very end of the night, when Seth and Stan struck gold.

CHAPTER SIX

"In the Name of the Father…"

Wanting to conduct an EVP session with just the two of them present, Seth and Stan went down into the basement and shut themselves in. Setting a digital voice recorder down on the ground between them, they sat on the floor and began to ask the usual EVP questions.

"Can you knock on something?" Stan asked, not really expecting a response. He got one anyway. There came the sound of movement from right outside the room. When Stan stuck his head around the door and swept the area with his flashlight, nobody was out there.

"What do you think that was?" Seth wondered.

"It sounded like a door opening," Stan said, "but none of the other doors are open."

The sound appeared loud and clear on the audio recording when Seth played it back afterward. Unfortunately, the exact nature of it is impossible to determine. It could indeed be a door opening, but it could just as easily be the scrape of a shoe on the floor.

Recalling that the cemetery had had a section that was specifically set aside for Catholics, Stan decided to try and reach out to them. In a clear, loud voice, he said, "In nomine Patris et Filii et Spiritus Sancti," which is Latin for *In the name of the father, and of the son, and of the holy spirit.*

He was more than a little disappointed when there was no response.

The two investigators went back to their EVP session, letting it go on for a while longer. Despite their best efforts, it seemed that nothing wanted to interact with them.

It was only when Seth played back the recording days later, during the evidence review phase, that he discovered that somebody had answered Stan after all. As he sat listening to the raw audio with his headphones, Seth heard Stan finished speaking, followed by thirty seconds of absolute silence.

Then, an extremely quiet, soft male voice spoke a single word:

SILENCE.

Whether it was an acknowledgment that Stan had stopped talking, or a request for a longer period of silence, is hard to say. But what cannot be denied is that somebody spoke a single, hushed, yet crystal-clear word onto the recording that neither man heard with their own ears at the time it was made.

It only takes a single, clearly-enunciated word of an anomalous origin to be considered a Class A EVP, and that was exactly what Seth had captured in the basement of the Waring House.

Apparently, somebody down there didn't much care for their voices...

Sunrise wasn't far away by the time the security guard came to escort us out of the building. He locked the Waring House up for the night, set the alarm, and waved us off on our way with a cheerful, "Did you catch any ghosts?"

"Not this time." We were all a little disappointed. Seth and Stan didn't know about their EVP yet, and it looked as if the night was a complete bust. During the drive home, all that I could think about was the possibility that the Waring House wasn't nearly as haunted as its reputation made out. It had been so peaceful and calm in there that I could quite easily have curled up in a chair and taken a nap.

But, I reminded myself, there was a wealth of eyewitness testimony, much of it from some very credible sources: the staff themselves, including the security guards who spent time in the building late at night.

Perhaps we had simply been there on the wrong night, I thought, or taken the wrong mix of people. Maybe the weather conditions weren't right. Any one of a hundred factors could have been sufficiently 'off' to hinder our investigation.

By the time I pulled into my driveway, the sun was just coming up, and the birds were singing. I had also managed to talk myself into coming around 180 degrees in my line of thinking. Based on the track record of the location and the credibility of those who worked there, I was once more optimistic that the spirits of Denver Botanic Gardens might have been shy, but would hopefully put in an appearance or two over the space of our remaining three nights there.

As things turned out, I was grossly underestimating their willingness to interact with us.

We had just spent our last relatively uneventful night at the Waring House. Things were about to get significantly more active.

CHAPTER SEVEN
"Get Out!"

Our next overnight investigation at the Gardens took place on a weekend, long after the staff and visitors had gone home at the end of the day. A week had passed since our last visit, and we were all eager to see what the place had in store for us this time.

As paranormal investigators, we always try our best to keep our expectations low when we're visiting a haunted location. Some places can be very much 'feast or famine,' and just because you experience paranormal activity there one night, it does not necessarily mean that things will go the same way the next time you visit. On the flip side, after the relatively quiet night we had just spent there the week before, nobody was getting their hopes up this time.

Fortunately for us, we were wrong. Our third night was to be the most active yet. After taking into consideration the intriguing EVP which Seth had recorded during his basement session with Stan, I elected to once again return to the Waring House to see if we could do better.

This time, I had assembled a team of six people, a number that is firmly within the 'Goldilocks Zone' for a building the size of the Waring House. Six was not too many people, yet nor was it too few. To our chagrin, we had learned the week before that sound traveled very efficiently throughout the old house — in fact, much *too* efficiently — thanks to some truly interesting acoustics.

For example, one team had been conducting an EVP session sitting on the hidden staircase at the far end of the building, while the other was doing the same thing at the top of the main staircase over on the other side. Some sound still made its way between the two groups. Audio contamination would prove to be a real problem at the Waring House. Once the digital audio files were played back during the evidence review phase, the sounds of each other's distant voices had bled through onto the recording, picked up by our extremely sensitive microphones.

In order to address the issue, I determined at the outset that we would no longer conduct simultaneous sessions inside the Waring House. We needed to be absolutely sure that if something which seemed anomalous appeared on our recordings, that it wasn't simply noise contamination coming from a neighboring group. As the evening wore on, we would soon have reason to be grateful for adopting that particular strategy.

In addition to myself, I had four seasoned investigators and one rookie. My friend and colleague Jason had a career in the medical field, but had since given that up in order to become a stay-at-home dad to his newborn baby daughter, Regan. Jason's wife, Linda, had joined us at the Waring House investigation the week before, and was taking care of the baby tonight so that Jason could get out into the field again and experience the historic old house for himself. Staying out overnight on an investigation was also the closest thing to uninterrupted peace and quiet that he was likely to get for quite some time, and it was hardly surprising that he looked tired before the investigation had even begun.

Catlyn had been part of the team when we visited on night one, and was now returning for her first investigation of the Waring House. She was also instrumental in helping to train Shane, one of the team's newest probationary members, who had also been present during our first night at Denver Botanic Gardens and had taken the majority of our baseline photographs. Eager and enthusiastic, Shane had yet to personally experience anything that might be considered paranormal during any of the investigations that he had attended, and he was cautiously optimistic that tonight would be the night when all of that changed.

One of the principal skills that Shane brought to the team was photography. While the rest of us walked around to the front door in order to meet with the evening security guard, Shane began to make a slow circle of the building, carefully and methodically taking photographs every few feet, capturing every aspect of the exterior from as many angles as he could manage. It was a dark and overcast night, so all of those pictures had to be taken with a flash. That meant that any light anomalies that may show up in the pictures would have to be viewed with extreme skepticism, as the combination of flash photography and reflective surfaces (such as the many glass window panes in the Waring House) would be prone to throwing up a lot of false positives.

Randy and Robbin were our guest investigators of the night. They belonged to another team with which we often conducted joint investigations. They were both a key part of the BCPRS extended family, as far as we were concerned. We had been investigating haunted locations together for the past twelve years, and I was always happy to have their skills and expertise along to bolster those of my own team. A retired I.T. professional by trade, Randy was spending his well-earned retirement as both a clockmaker and as a paranormal investigator.

He was also a self-avowed 'gear-head,' and if there was a piece of technology that could be used for the purposes of investigating the paranormal, the chances were excellent that he owned at least one version of it, if not more — many of which were the earliest prototypes, often obtained before the devices ever became commercially available. That explained why he was lugging a series of heavy equipment cases along with him as we approached the front door.

Last but by no means least, Randy's wife Robbin was a nurse with many years of experience in the medical field, ranging from emergency medicine to end of life care. She was limping along behind Randy, slowed down by a recently-broken toe. Robbin wasn't the sort to let a minor injury keep her from attending a field investigation, however, and I was impressed by the fact that she didn't complain about the pain even once during the course of the night. She had spent many years developing her mediumistic skills and psychic sensitivities. Her extra-sensory impressions sometimes yielded valuable information during our cases, particularly when they could be backed up with other, more tangible evidence, such as EVP recordings, that corroborated her own findings.

Michael, the security guard on duty that evening,

unlocked the door promptly at 7:30pm and allowed us access to the property. He was a little surprised when we turned up, as nobody had let him know of our visit in advance, but after a short phone call to confirm that we did actually have permission, he was more than happy to let us in, and even gave us an impromptu guided tour of the house, pointing out some of its spookier highlights.

We began at the foot of the main staircase.

"One night, an employee was coming down this staircase and was heading home," Michael said. "She was looking in through the open doors of the dining room, and told me that she saw a bright ball of light drifting through the air in there. It passed across the room and just disappeared."

I made a mental note to try and debunk that later.

Then he led us upstairs. The glass door that led to the director's office was closed and locked. By prior agreement, we had declared this area out of bounds.

As we toured the remainder of the upper floor, all of which was open to us, Michael recounted the events of an evening not so long ago, when he was making his rounds before locking up the Waring House for the night. He had noticed that one particular employee was in a very obvious hurry to collect all of her things and leave.

"You don't have to rush. There's plenty of time," Michael told her. He would be on duty until eleven o'clock that night, so there was no need for the lady to hurry out the door.

"No," she replied, glancing nervously at a clock on the wall, "I have to be out of here by seven o'clock. *Have* to be."

Beginning to get a little curious now, Michael asked her what was so urgent that she must leave the building by seven. Perhaps a scheduled appointment? But she went on to explain that the last time she had worked this late at her desk, she had very distinctly heard a menacing voice growl at her: *"Get out!"*

"I've never experienced anything like that here myself," Michael shrugged, "but that lady was adamant that she wasn't going to stay past seven, so I escorted her out and locked the building up behind us both."

His anecdote piqued my interest greatly, not least because I'd heard a very similar story before from a different employee. The reader may recall that when we investigated the Boettcher Conservatory and its surrounding facilities, I'd spoken with Rose, a member of the cleaning staff. She had been cleaning the ladies' locker room, when she had heard the voice of a younger girl quite clearly telling her to *"Get me out of here!"* While the voice in this particular instance was female, we don't know the gender of the disembodied voice heard by the lady who wanted to leave by seven o'clock, as she didn't volunteer that information to Michael.

Could it have been the same entity speaking in both cases? It is certainly possible. The two locations are separated by just a few hundred feet. Then again, it is equally possible that two different entities made themselves known, though if so, they appear to have had different agendas. In one instance, the entity was telling the employee to get out, expressing a desire to be left alone; in the other, the female voice seemed to be making a plea for rescue, asking Rose to "get *me* out." Based on this comparison, not to mention the fact that the voices had been heard in different parts of the botanic gardens, I considered it more likely that we were dealing with two different entities.

Michael led us back downstairs and into the kitchen, which still had a number of its original fixtures and fittings. One thing that had intrigued us all on our first visit was the old intercom box and the electric clock which were mounted above one another on a wall between two doorways. The clock read 1-2-3-4, as did an identical model located in an upstairs corridor.

"I was in here one day, and I very distinctly heard that thing buzz," Michael said, indicating the clock. "I wasn't hearing things. It buzzed. A couple of times, in fact."

The security guard reached out to lift two strands of wire which were dangling from beneath the unit. "That shouldn't be possible," he went on. "The wires were cut a long time ago. There's no power running to the device at all."

Frowning, Catlyn ran a tri-field EMF meter over the intercom and the clock. This device measures levels of electromagnetic energy across multiple directions simultaneously, and offers significantly more accurate readings than the cheaper, more ubiquitous models such as the K-2 meter.

It didn't take long for Catlyn to conclusively determine that both devices *and* the entire section of the wall upon which they were mounted were completely inert — electromagnetically speaking, at least.

I relayed to everyone what I had been told by the director, Brian, when he had given me my first daytime walk-through of the house. He had also personally experienced the two bells on top of the intercom unit ringing of their own accord, as though somebody from a bygone age was attempting to call through to the kitchen and place an order for food. As with the electric clock, the power wires dangled uselessly. The intercom had not been capable of receiving power for quite a few years now, and there should have been no way that the bells could have rung.

Although we had tried (unsuccessfully) to debunk this phenomenon during our last visit, I had a different set of investigators with me this time, and wanted to give them the opportunity to try and find a non-paranormal explanation for themselves, rather than just taking my word for it. Their attempts to explain Brian's experience rationally involved blowing on the bells as hard as they possibly could. The directed air current did evoke a very, *very* weak chime from them, something we hadn't achieved before, but the sound wasn't remotely as distinct as that which Brian had described.

We also had to consider the fact that there had been no windows or doors open at the time Mike had heard the bells ring, and as we proved during our baseline testing using hanging sheets and strips of paper, the Waring House is not a particularly drafty one. My colleagues also tried thumping and slamming the wall, then jumping vigorously up and down next to it, in order to create vibrations that would travel up the length of the wood. Once again, they were unable to make the bells ring in this manner, which meant that we had failed at finding an obvious explanation with which to debunk the phenomenon.

"Well, if there's nothing else I can do for you, I'll lock you guys in for the night," Michael told us. We confirmed that there wasn't, and thanked him for his time. There were handshakes all round, and then he returned to the main building for the remainder of his shift, promising to inform the oncoming late-night security guard of our presence inside the house. The entrances and exits were all secured behind him, ensuring that if we *were* to be disturbed over the course of the night, then at least it wouldn't be by any flesh and blood intruder — unless somebody physically broke in.

We went back out into the main lobby again.

"I want that thing so badly," Randy practically drooled, staring at the beautiful and ornate grandfather clock that sits at the foot of the main staircase in the manner of a starving dog eyeing up a cut of prime steak. With a twinkle in his eye, he asked playfully, "Who's going to help me load it up into the bed of my truck? I need some volunteers…"

I swatted him lightly on the arm. "What a *great* way to make sure we never get invited back here again in future. Still, it *is* a beautiful piece of craftsmanship."

The first order of business was unpacking our equipment and getting everything set up. This took place in the great hall, just as it had the week before. There was ample table space in there, and as it was relatively central, we could respond to any part of the house in a hurry if we thought that something unusual was taking place. It made for the perfect operations center.

Once our gear was laid out and ready for use, I wanted to try and debunk the "floating ball of light" that Michael had told us about. The dining room is an absolutely beautiful piece of architectural design, paneled in rich dark woods and inlaid with elegant glass windows. As mentioned earlier, I've learned over the course of my career in paranormal research (sometimes the hard way) to distrust reports of 'light anomalies' in places where a great deal of glass is present – and the dining room had many windows.

My first thought was that the witness could have misinterpreted the light of passing car headlights, especially if they were on the 'high beam' setting, when they passed through one or multiple window panes, and then refracted, creating a brief optical illusion. I'd seen a similar effect take place in a bar located in my adopted home town of Longmont (see my book *Haunted Longmont,* published in

2015 by The History Press, for the full story) in which the rays of the sun would shine through several sets of glass doors and windows, before bouncing off the mirror behind the back of the bar, thereby creating the illusion of a ghostly bartender standing behind the bar itself.

It only happened at a specific time of the day, when the sun was at just the right angle in the sky, and did not occur when the sky was cloudy or dim. It just so happened that the eyewitnesses in that particular case were coming in to work at precisely the right time, on precisely the right day (in terms of the weather conditions) and were seeing *their own reflection,* mistaking it for a phantom bartender. Could something similar have happened here at the Waring House?

It was a possibility that we would have to investigate thoroughly before even contemplating a paranormal explanation.

Both York Street and 9th Avenue were fairly busy, heavily-trafficked roads, even at eight o'clock in the evening. We took turns positioning ourselves at various points on the staircase, and looked in through the open doors of the dining room. Thanks to the near-constant stream of vehicles passing by outside, it didn't take long for us to rule out the possibility of it having been either car or truck headlights that had created the floating ball of light effect. Nothing remotely comparable was seen by any of us, no matter where we stood on the staircase or in the lobby.

For the next stage of our experiment, Catlyn gamely volunteered her services. She ventured out into the chilly February night air armed only with a high-powered flashlight. Catlyn worked her way around the front of the house, moving slowly from left to right, shining the beam in through the windows at various angles and heights. Sometimes she was crouching, sometimes walking normally, and at others she was standing on tiptoe, directing the flashlight beam through each pane of glass at every conceivable angle, making sure that she also shone it through multiple sets of windows wherever possible.

The end result: There was nothing remotely like the drifting light anomaly that the employee had described to Michael. Unless it had been entirely a product of her imagination (something that we could never entirely rule out, given the many stories about the haunting of the Waring House that have been passed on from one employee to the next over the years) then we were at a loss to explain her sighting…in conventional terms, at least.

Still optimistic about the night that lay ahead of us, we

settled down to the business of conducting our investigation. I gave the rest of the team a quick tour of the house, focusing on the areas that Michael hadn't taken us to. I made a point of emphasizing the areas where I'd been told that certain paranormal phenomena had taken place in the past. I have to admit that it was a great deal of fun taking them into the open office section that was directly adjacent to the great hall, telling them that there was a hidden staircase, and challenging them to go and find it.

The team didn't have to search for too long before they discovered the hinged bookcase that served as a doorway. There were appreciative sounds of delight when the door swung open smoothly, revealing the hidden back staircase. Jason spoke for everybody when he said the same thing I had thought when first discovering it for myself: "It feels like we're in an episode of *Scooby Doo*!"

It was hard to disagree. Bookcases that swung open to reveal hidden staircases, which in turn concealed secret crawlspaces, were pretty cool not matter how you looked at things. I had investigated more than my fair share of castles and historic buildings in my time, but this was a first for me.

"You ain't seen nothing yet," I chuckled, squatting down to grasp the bottom step. I didn't have to apply much pressure in order to get it to swing upward, revealing the hidden crawlspace beneath.

We had only conducted a single EVP session on that staircase during the previous night of investigation, which I didn't really think was enough time to do it justice. The rest of the team agreed, and so we resolved to give it a little more time and attention later on that night.

While the rest of the team went back to the main hall in order to select our equipment for the first investigative session, Catlyn went to answer the call of nature. The ground floor restroom inside the Waring House is located in the lobby, off to the left when one enters through the front door, just past the main staircase.

Catlyn had only been inside the restroom for a few minutes when we all heard a tremendous rattling noise coming from that direction. It sounded as if somebody was vigorously jiggling the door handle, trying their hardest to get out. We shrugged, thinking that she was probably having a slight problem unlocking the door from the inside, and would call out for help if she really needed it.

We heard the door open. Catlyn stepped back into the Great Hall. Looking and sounding somewhat less than thrilled, she wanted to know who had been trying to get into the restroom – after all, hadn't we known that she was in there? The rest of the team looked at one another in confusion.

"None of us came over there," Jason told her. "Everybody has been sitting right here, checking our equipment."

Catlyn's face may have lost a little bit of color when the implications of that statement sank in. Once again, we went around and checked the doors, making sure that we were completely alone inside the big, old house. Of course, we knew that we wouldn't find anybody. What were the odds that somebody would be able to get through one of the locked doors, creep up to the restroom in complete silence, play a practical joke on Catlyn, and then make a getaway, all without one of us seeing or hearing them?

Whoever or whatever it was that had rattled the bathroom door so aggressively, it certainly could not have been a flesh and blood human being.

Carefully and methodically, we set about trying to debunk the strange occurrence. Some kind of natural vibration, perhaps from a passing vehicle or minor earth tremor, was out. We were using a device which sensed and recorded vibrations, and it wasn't picking up any tremors at all.

What about some kind of random breeze or wind gust? We didn't detect anything of the kind. There were no drafts coming in through any of the doors and windows (all of which were closed anyway) that might explain away what had just happened.

Ultimately, we were forced to conclude that the door had been shaken by something that we just couldn't see. Murphy's Law was in full effect, which meant that, of course, NONE of our array of cameras happened to be covering that restroom door. On the other hand, our audio recorders *did* pick up the sound of the door rattling. It lasted for no more than three seconds, and was not preceded by footsteps or any other noises that might suggest the presence of a human intruder.

To quote Sherlock Holmes, it felt as if the game was now afoot, and there was a palpable air of excitement when the team headed off for our first location: the basement. We used a variety of different instruments during this first session. One of the more controversial was the Phasma Box, a piece of Instrumental Trans-Communication (ITC) software that, some claim, discarnate entities can use to communicate with us. Quite often, the Phasma Box generates nothing more than senseless gibberish, but every so often it will spit out something that appears to be genuinely meaningful.

At Denver Botanic Gardens, the intelligent responses would soon begin to arrive thick and fast, particularly when we were working downstairs in the basement.

CHAPTER EIGHT
"IN A MASS GRAVE."

Randy was both the owner and the operator of the Phasma Box. It was running on his laptop computer, hooked up to an external speaker. He had it working in no time, and we all gathered round in the dark expectantly. Most ITC devices take a little time to 'warm up,' so to speak, usually requiring at least a few minutes in order to shake themselves out and begin making any kind of sense. Not so in the cellar of the Waring House. Whoever or whatever was active down there seemed only too eager to communicate with us.

ITC sessions generally start off with a few standard test questions, just to get the ball rolling, such as asking whether there are any spirits present who wished to talk with us, and then asking a little bit about themselves and their background.

Chilly wind, said a male-sounding voice. Considering that the weather was freezing cold, not to mention the fact that we could hear the wind howling around the eaves of the house, I was willing to call that first statement a hit. Needless to say, I would have been considerably less impressed if the Phasma Box had said the exact same thing on a hot, still evening in July rather than a cold night in February. These are the kind of things that ought to confound the arguments of those skeptics who insist that nothing meaningful comes through ITC devices such as this, and that every such 'communication' is nothing more than audible pareidolia, the human brain tricking itself into thinking that it hears something meaningful in what is actually nothing more than a random jumble of noises.

If a statement made by a voice from the Phasma Box (or any other purported spirit communication device) could be corroborated by something objective from the outside world — in this case, the fact that the night was both chilly and windy — then it made for rather compelling evidence, in my opinion.

After this promising start, things suddenly took a turn toward the nasty. Robbin took her turn asking a few questions, enquiring whether the spirits had to remain down there in the basement or whether they were able to move around the house and gardens.

Another male voice, different in tone and timbre from the first, jumped in and replied to her with a shocking obscenity:

YOU C—-!

We were all taken aback by this sudden, unexpected burst of verbal abuse. Robbin had been speaking politely and respectfully, fully aware that we were operating on what was, for all intents and purposes, sacred ground. Because of this, the entire team had agreed that no provocative or antagonistic questioning techniques were going to be used. Disrespecting spirit entities is almost always a bad idea (not to mention just plain bad form) and while it can yield results, sometimes those results are not the kind that you want. I have personally seen scratches and other physical injuries ensue because a paranormal investigator got a little too big for his or her boots and decided to mouth off to the spirits during an ITC session.

Robbin, however, had been the very model of politeness and professionalism. She certainly had not done anything to deserve being called such a name. The EVP was a Class A, clear-as-day voice, and was delivered in a cold, almost laconic manner. We could all agree that any entity which was willing to use the 'C' word to describe a lady — especially when such an insult was completely unprovoked — probably wasn't going to be very nice, and wouldn't have our best interests at heart. It made us resolve to be very careful about our future line of questioning.

A few seconds later, a female voice piped up to say, *We're Catholic*. This voice spoke a little more rapidly than that of the abusive male, but the words were still extremely clear. Considering that a large section of the old Mount Calvary cemetery had indeed been set aside for those were Catholic, I thought that this was an intriguing potential hit as well.

Next up, *It's a chilly wind* came through the box a second time, every bit as clear and distinct as it had been just a few minutes before. Note that this time, two extra words — *It's a* — were added to the beginning of the sentence. This was the same voice that had spoken the first time, and it had the bland, almost robotic quality to it that one often hears on EVP recordings. It sounded almost as if the words were coming through an artificial voice synthesizer. This occurs not only on ITCs that are captured via a computer app, but also those that are imprinted directly on magnetic tape or the drive of a digital voice recorder.

Some ITC researchers have theorized that the synthesized nature of these voices may be a by-product of the manner in which verbal communication occurs between their dimension or plane of reality and our own. This is an intriguing hypothesis, and one that merits a great deal more research.

Our questioning continued without much in the way of meaningful results for a while, yielding nothing more than random sounds and audio fragments. Then Robbin asked how many spirits were down there in the basement with us, and a husky female voice intoned the word, *Eighteen*.

We looked around at one another in the near-darkness, on the off-chance that we might actually catch sight of one of those eighteen spirit entities who, the voice claimed, were crowded in there with us. If there were any shadow figures keeping us company down there, then unfortunately none of us saw them.

Still, it wasn't all that difficult to believe that there might be a large number of entities clustered around us. The ground that surrounded us contained hundreds, no, *thousands* of bodies, every one of which lay in a grave that was now long since forgotten. It didn't stretch the bounds of credibility to imagine that there might be hundreds of restless souls still earthbound in the area, perhaps incensed at the notion of what had happened to their final resting place. The man who had sworn at Robbin certainly hadn't been happy, and from what was said next, it seemed that another male spirit was also displeased with our presence.

GET OUT! yelled an angry male voice. We began to shift a little uncomfortably. That was the second negative message we had gotten, and it was becoming difficult to avoid coming to the conclusion that we might not be very welcome down in that basement. This was the same phrase that had been yelled at the employee some months earlier.

I will freely admit that in cases such as this, the mind also has a tendency to play tricks. Having a fertile imagination can sometimes be a detriment rather than a benefit, because I suddenly began to conjure up images of skeletal human remains packed three to a coffin in the earth on all sides of us and beneath the floor on which we sat. Considering the number of coffin samples that the engineers had encountered during their test drilling in 1973, there was actually a fairly good chance that we really were within five or six feet of several undiscovered graves. It really was a chilling thought, but it was nothing in comparison to what was to come next.

"Do you live here, or do you work here?" Robbin asked, trying to get a better handle on the identity of our invisible communicator. The voice which responded was definitely male, and said four words that shocked us all.

In a mass grave.

"Did it just say 'In a mass grave?'" Jason repeated, unable to believe his ears. On playback, we confirmed that this was *exactly* what had been said. If there was a more apt description of what lay beneath the Waring House and the grounds that surrounded it, I would be hard-pressed to think of one. It was all, technically speaking, one big, scattered mass grave.

Once again, the ITC application was stretching the boundaries of coincidence to their breaking point, as far as I was concerned. Yes, certain words and phrases could be expected to pop up from time to time that might generally apply to the current situation (that's how most horoscopes work, after all) but this was so specific, so apropos to the cellar of the Waring House, that the team were all in agreement: this couldn't be seen as anything other than a direct hit, and a bullseye at that.

It was hard to escape the conclusion that we were in contact with *something* intelligent, based upon the results of our question and answer session. The great question now was, who — or possibly *what* — was talking back to us?

After having some success down in the basement, we relocated to the back staircase to try our luck there. Unfortunately, whoever had been speaking to us downstairs didn't seem willing to tag along, because all of our equipment remained obstinately silent.

With the night wearing on, we were all starting to get a little tired. On an investigation where nothing had been happening, I would already have called it a night by now. But the results of the Phasma Box session we had conducted down in the basement were fascinating, and we were all excited and eager to keep going. Ten minutes for some caffeine and a snack were all that it took before my fellow investigators and I were ready to give the app another try, though this time we planned to relocate to the dining room upstairs.

The team gathered around the long wooden table. Randy had already hooked up the laptop and fired up the Phasma Box again. As we took our seats, setting down recording equipment, EMF meters and thermometers on top of the table, the sense of anticipation we felt was almost tangible.

Once again, the Phasma Box seemed to require almost nothing in the way of a warm-up period. After asking whether there were any spirits present that would like to communicate with us, I jumped straight in with a question about whether they liked it in the Waring House or not. The voice that answered me sounded like that of a very aristocratic, upper-class English female.

No, I don't, the voice said haughtily, reminding me of old recordings that I had heard of the Queen of England. In my neck of the woods, this type of speech pattern is sometimes referred to as 'BBC English,' which certainly made sense, historically speaking. I recalled the fact that Colorado did not lack for English visitors in the late 1800s. Many came for the hunting, fishing, and outdoor life. Could this be one of them?

Take, for example, Windham Wyndham-Quin, otherwise known as the 4th Earl of Dunraven. This wealthy Anglo-Irish aristocrat passed through Denver in 1872, with a view to hunting buffalo. Lord Dunraven purchased vast tracts of land in the area that is now home to the town of Estes Park, and opened his 'English Hotel' just east of the township. (At the nearby Stanley Hotel, Room 401, named after Lord Dunraven, is widely regarded as one of its most haunted).

Whoever this English-sounding lady was, she could very easily have been a visiting Briton who perhaps died during her foreign adventure and was subsequently buried in the old Denver cemetery. In some cases, spirits seem to return to those places in which they were happiest during their lifetimes. This is one possible reason why the aforementioned Stanley Hotel is believed to have more than its fair share of ghosts.

The Stanley has given joy and happiness to countless visitors for more than a hundred years, and where one finds strong emotions (whether positive or negative), ghosts are usually not far behind. This explanation wouldn't seem to apply to the Waring House, however, because the words, *No I don't,* were spoken most emphatically.

Sadly, the unknown lady's identity remained a mystery, as she did not speak to us again during that particular recording session...but, unbeknownst to us, we would hear from a similar-sounding communicator later on.

A few minutes later, Catlyn heard what she thought may have been her name. This is a fairly common occurrence when engaging in ITC — and tends to be a little creepy — and so she politely requested that her name be repeated. A harsh, guttural voice growled back: *OUT NOW!*

Yet another suggestion that we might be unwelcome visitors! The voice wasn't dissimilar to the one that had told us to get out of the cellar a short while earlier, and both speakers sounded male, with an angry, glottic tone to them. This instruction for visitors (including employees) to get out of the Waring House was starting to become a theme.

There was no question of stopping now. These results had given our team a second wind, and now all of us wanted to push on and see what more we could discover. With hindsight, it's a good thing that we did, because we were about to experience one of the more remarkable aspects of ITC experimentation. Pioneers in the field of ITC research have reported a highly unusual phenomenon that goes all the way back to its very earliest days. In some cases, as the person who is asking questions starts to speak, the answer to their question is delivered before they can even finish their sentence. This strongly suggests that a type of telepathy may be at work, as the full question appears to be plucked directly from their mind and immediately answered in the form of an EVP.

That is exactly what happened to me when I asked my next question.

"Did they relocate your body to another cemetery?" I asked, but my sentence was interrupted with the word *Evergreen*.

On the recording, the Q & A sounds like this: "Did they relocate your body to *EVERGREEN* another cemetery?" The phantom voice, which once again has that unusually atonal and flat quality to it, speaks directly over the top of my own voice.

From our historical research, we knew that a number of the bodies were relocated from Mount Pleasant Cemetery to Mount Olivet Cemetery in nearby Wheat Ridge, but Colorado also has a number of Evergreen Cemeteries, in places such as Colorado Springs (dating to 1871) and Leadville (1879). Could it be that we were speaking with a spirit whose body was taken to one of those places instead of to Mount Olivet? The possibility was certainly intriguing.

"Can you say hello to Richard?" Robbin asked, pointing in my direction. A good twenty seconds went by before a distorted, garbled male voice slurred the word *Richard*

I have replayed this particular section of the recording back many times, listening to it over and over with noise-canceling headphones. One pitfall of analyzing suspected ITC messages is that there is a tendency to hear what one wants or expects to hear. Psychologically speaking, we are all the star of our own internal movie, and it can be immensely flattering (albeit a little frightening sometimes) for an EVP to speak your name. Nevertheless, it does appear that this is exactly what happened in this instance.

This has happened to me before at several other haunted locations, most notably at the old Tooele Valley Hospital in

Utah, which has since become a full contact haunted house attraction named Asylum 49. My name once emerged from an SB-7 spirit box during a particularly heated session outside one of the most active rooms, that of an Alzheimer's patient named Westley.

When investigating the infamous Black Monk house in Pontefract, England (the site of what many believe to be the most violent and long-lasting poltergeist case on record) my name once again came through the speaker of a similar device. That instance was particularly unique because both my first *and* my last name were spoken, something that I had never heard of happening before. In fact, it was so surprising that I immediately became suspicious, thinking something along the lines of, "if it seems too good to be true, then it most likely *is.*" I suspected that the spirit box in question could be monitoring the conversations taking place in its immediate vicinity, recording the words that were spoken, and playing them back in the guise of so-called EVPs. The only fly in that particular ointment was that when I played back the raw audio recordings from the moment that the box was switched on, at no point did anybody *ever* mention my last name in conversation.

Hopefully, we would hear some of the other

investigators' names spoken through the Phasma Box. If so, it would strengthen the supporting evidence enormously.

As the Phasma Box session continued, one of the investigators asked whether there was anything that we could do for the spirits of the gardens. The response, delivered in a stern male voice, was both rapid and unequivocal.

Some respect.

"We respect you," Jason reassured the invisible speaker, who had sounded rather annoyed, based upon the tone of his voice.

Apparently, the communicators were not all that convinced by Jason's assertion, because the output from the Phasma Box soon devolved into a mix of random noise and atonal garbage. We counted ourselves lucky to have gotten such a broad range of intelligent responses, and I was already looking forward to poring over them again and again during the evidence review phase of the investigation, which would begin just as soon as we had all gotten some sleep.

Interestingly enough, once it came time to review the recordings, Randy and Robbin were thrilled to discover that we appeared to have been joined by yet another invisible guest. They were analyzing the raw audio recordings from our dining room Phasma Box session. Right at the very beginning, just as the investigators and I were all taking our seats, came the sound of a young boy. He spoke only two words.

Hi, Mommy.

When they sent the file to me for review, I listened to it with a set of noise-canceling headphones and the volume cranked all the way up. Sure enough, there it was. The high-pitched voice was far too young to be that of an adult (certainly not anybody who was physically present in either of our two Phasma Box sessions from that night) and spoke only once. Once he had greeted his mother, the boy was never heard from again.

The recording had been made when we were sitting down around the table in the upstairs meeting room, only a few feet away from the restroom where Catlyn had been the victim of the door-rattling prank. Could it be that we had recorded the sound of the young lad who was said to roam the Waring House, looking for people to take part in his fun and games? It was a definitely possible, and we had no better working hypothesis for how a boy's voice could have turned up on that recording.

Once again, the Waring House had delivered on its

potential.

After a break and some light refreshments, we decided to try our luck with the main staircase once again. Choosing spots at the top of the landing, we spread out and set up our sensing equipment, then proceeded to run a lights-out EVP session.

Although we didn't get any EVPs during this particular session, we all heard the sound of footsteps walking around on the second floor, in the darkness of the back hallway. Whenever an investigator went to check on the source of the sounds, however, they would suddenly stop. It was a frustrating game of cat and mouse, one that we grew tired of fairly quickly.

The remainder of the night was quiet, and try as we might, we were unable to get anything in the way of substantive results.

Yet I was now totally convinced of the validity of the haunting. We had gotten enough evidence to prove that to our own satisfaction, and were looking forward to delving even further into the mysteries of the Waring House.

CHAPTER NINE
Demon

More than a year would pass before we returned to Denver Botanic Gardens to continue our research. This gap in the investigation was almost entirely my fault. My case load had gotten extremely busy, and I'd visited a number of bucket list locations over that period that I simply couldn't turn down. These included Gettysburg, the Cage (a prison for those accused of witchcraft), the London Underground, Iowa's notorious haunted Malvern Manor, and many others.

My work had also been featured on a couple of TV shows, *Haunted Case Files* and *Haunted Hospitals,* and I'd taken a part-time job giving ghost tours at the Stanley Hotel, inspiration for Stephen King's *The Shining,* and also, for my money, the most haunted hotel in America…if not the world.

So, I'd been a busy bee, but the botanic gardens were always there, lurking in the back of my mind. This case truly constituted unfinished business, and I was convinced that we could definitely capture more evidence there if the opportunity presented itself.

The powers that be graciously granted permission for two more nights of research, and once again arranged for the security team to give us overnight access. This time, I wanted to focus one hundred percent of our time and attention on the Waring House, as I was now certain that it was the most active part of the entire facility.

Our first investigations had taken place in the early springtime, and it had been pretty cold outside. Now we were returning at the end of summer, when the weather was warmer. I wondered if this would have any effect at all on the level of paranormal activity that we encountered.

Only time would tell.

Our first overnight investigation began at ten o'clock in the evening, a little over an hour after the last of the visitors and staff had left the botanic gardens for the night. It was late August, and the air was seasonably warm — T-shirt weather, as I liked to think of it.

Pulling up to the concrete parking structure on the opposite side of York Street, I saw that I was the last member of our team to arrive. The rest of the investigators had congregated around their cars, chatting and laughing with one another. They were from a sister team named AAPI, the American Association of Paranormal

Investigators.

I had worked with them on numerous cases over the past ten years, and we had built up a good working relationship. Our personal philosophies and investigative styles were very similar, as were our senses of humor, and I wanted to get a fresh take on the activity at Denver Botanic Gardens.

Their fearless leader, Stephen, was a Catholic priest, professional cellist, and a seasoned paranormal investigator of long standing. He was also a good friend of mine, and the first guy I had called when I picked up some kind of attachment at a haunted location and brought it home with me.

Bizarre things had begun to happen around my house. Both my wife and I saw shadow figures. The Christmas lights took to switching themselves off and on of their own volition. A woman's voice was heard, calling out from downstairs and driving my dog, Greta, absolutely bonkers because there was nobody to be seen when she went pounding down the staircase to find whoever it was that had spoken.

The very last straw was when a number of framed pictures flew off the mantelpiece and smashed on the ground, narrowly missing my cat, Vlad, by a hair's breadth.

Quite understandably, my wife declared that enough was enough, and despite my being an agnostic (I like to think of myself as being spiritual but not religious) I called upon my favorite Catholic priest, who wasted no time in coming over and performing an extensive blessing on our home. I liked to think of it as calling in the spiritual heavy artillery.

After the ritual was completed, our home was free of paranormal disturbances, and we thanked Stephen with a hearty home-cooked dinner.

Stephen's colleagues Jill, Erik, and Richard had also accompanied him. It was their first time investigating at the botanic gardens, and they were excited to see what the night ahead had in store. I knew exactly how they felt. There was something about this location that intrigued and fascinated me, and I clearly wasn't the only one.

We all exchanged hugs and hellos. As the AAPI team began unloading cases full of equipment from their cars, I called the security hotline. It had been arranged in advance that we would start our investigation at ten o'clock, which was just five minutes away.

"Hello?" a female voice said at the other end of the line.

"Denver Botanic Gardens Security."

I explained who I was, and asked to be let into the

Waring House. The lady sounded puzzled. She had no idea that we were supposed to be there tonight, she said, and told me that she would make a phone call and get back to me.

Slightly concerned, I stood there and shot the breeze with the AAPI crew. In the back of my mind, I was hoping that the mix-up would get sorted out quickly, because we were burning investigation time. Fortunately, the matter was soon resolved — it had been nothing more than a simple communications snafu — and Lisa, the security guard on duty that night, said that she'd meet us at the group entrance to the botanic gardens.

True to her word, she was waiting for us when we crossed the street. Laughing about the initial confusion, we fell into conversation as she led us along the path toward the rear of the Waring House. Cheerful and friendly, Lisa was only too happy to answer my questions, including the one about whether she had experienced anything strange during her time at the botanic gardens.

"I've only been working here for three weeks, on the swing shift," she chuckled, "but I've heard the stories. We've *all* heard the stories! I don't mind if anything spooky happens to me. In fact, I think it'd be cool if it did."

Lisa hadn't known that there would be visitors spending

the night in the Waring House, so she had switched off all the lights earlier in the evening and locked the building up tight. No sooner had she told us this than we rounded the final corner, and Lisa saw something that stopped her dead in her tracks.

Lights were shining brightly in several of the upstairs and downstairs windows of the house.

"That ain't right," she said, shaking her head. "*I know* I switched them all off before!"

As a paramedic, I get lied to for a living. A LOT. As such, I've developed a pretty good radar for when somebody is trying to put one over on me. I wasn't getting any such vibe from Lisa. Her tone, body language, and general affect all seemed completely genuine to me.

The AAPI crew were all grinning, happy to see that things were off and running. We hadn't even stepped foot in the building yet, and already strange things were afoot. We were all hoping that this boded well for the coming evening's investigation.

Lisa, who just moments before had been saying how cool it would be to have a paranormal experience, seemed to have undergone the world's fastest change of heart. Hastily, she unlocked the back door to the Waring House and ushered us through.

We trooped inside. Lisa wasted no time in closing the door, locking us in, and then disappeared off into the night without so much as a wave goodbye. Her enthusiasm for a 'cool paranormal encounter' had been replaced with an urge to put some space between her and the historic old house as quickly as possible.

It looked as if, once again, our old friend the Waring House wasn't going to let us down.

The lights in the lobby, on the staircase, and in most of the upstairs rooms had indeed been switched on. We walked around the house, making sure that all of the windows and doors were closed and secured.

Many paranormal investigators have a bit of the inner control freak about them, particularly when it comes to the environment in which they are investigating. We carefully noted the position of the light switches and which doors were open.

"Hey, quit it!" Stephen snapped irritably. We all turned to look at him. He was walking out of the dining room, heading in the direction of the lobby, and had stopped dead in his tracks.

"What?" Erik wanted to know.

Stephen raised a hand to the back of his head. "Somebody just pulled my hair. Well, the one hair I have left, anyway...gave the hair on top of my head a sharp tug."

There was nobody within touching distance of him at the time, but Stephen was adamant that he had felt it happen. Erik and Jill stepped away, saying that they wanted to wander around the building for a while and get a sense of things. Both profess to have a degree of psychic sensitivity, something that I had seen validated first hand on other investigations. In the past, they had both demonstrated an ability to pinpoint potential hot spots at a haunted location that sometimes bordered on the uncanny.

While they were gone, the rest of us set about unpacking more of our equipment, and making sure that the batteries were fresh in each device. The pair returned ten minutes later.

"Find anything?" I asked. It was difficult to keep the eagerness out of my voice.

"There's something strange going on in that copier room," Erik said, meaning the photocopier room upstairs that faced out onto 9th Avenue.

"The energies in there are something else," Jill agreed. "It would be a good idea to spend some time in there tonight."

I trusted their instincts implicitly, and immediately resolved to focus on the copier room right from the outset. The entire team went upstairs to the second floor. Erik urged us to begin with an EVP session in that room, so that's exactly what we started out with.

It turned out to be a great call on his part.

We all squeezed into the copier room, each of us finding somewhere comfortable to sit or stand as best we could. While we each took out our cell phones and set them to airplane mode, Erik explained that he could feel that some type of energy was present in the room with us.

"What's it doing?" I asked, looking around. To me, it just seemed like an ordinary photocopier room.

"Just hanging out in here, not doing much of anything," he said. He wasn't sensing anything negative or malicious about our invisible companion. In his words, it was simply "chilling out," waiting to see what we were going to do.

Three digital voice recorders were started running, set down at roughly equidistant points around the room. Erik explained what the purpose of the recorders was to whatever energy form was present, and then we launched right into the EVP session.

The mood was light-hearted and jovial. We took our role as paranormal investigators seriously, but not *too* seriously — there's a lot to be said for bringing a little levity to field research. We've discovered after a lot of trial and error that sometimes, you get better results when the team is kidding around a little, perhaps because of the more positive energy that laughter and humor brings along with it. We don't know exactly *how* that works, only that for whatever reason, it does.

Rather than ask the standard EVP questions requesting that the spirits speak their name, when they died, and various other identifying pieces of information, Erik went with something rather less conventional.

"Can you say, 'Bean burrito?'"

"Can you say, 'C'mon, Stewie?'" I chimed in. Erik rolled his eyes. For the longest time, I have taken great delight in pointing out that Erik's natural speaking voice sounds uncannily like that of Brian Griffin, the dog from the TV show *Family Guy*, as voiced by its creator, Seth MacFarlane. I never missed an opportunity to put in a reference to *Family Guy*, and luckily for me, the good-natured Erik tolerated it with grace and humor.

We didn't hear anything unusual during the session. Opting to keep the first session short, Erik stopped recording after less than a minute (this technique is called the 'Burst EVP method') and hooked the recorder up to an external speaker.

He hit the play button. Erik's voice filled the room.

"Can you say, 'bean burrito?'"

Nothing.

"Can you say, 'C'mon Stewie?'"

Apparently, our unseen visitor wasn't interested in saying either of those things. What he *did* say, however, was something far more exciting.

There was a whisper on the audio recording. Faint, hard to hear, but undeniably there nonetheless. I plugged in a set of noise-cancelling headphones, cranked up the volume, and had another listen.

My jaw dropped.

"What did it say?" Erik asked. Wordlessly, I handed him the headphones, then watched his eyebrows raise in surprise. Jill was next. Eventually, everybody took a turn listening.

This was a Class C EVP, difficult to make out clearly without headphones, and challenging to identify the exact words spoken even with their help. Nevertheless, our recorders had captured the sound of a man whispering.

He spoke only a single word.

Demon.

CHAPTER TEN
The Devil's Toybox

In the lexicon of paranormal research, there is no more contentious word than 'demon.' Practically every investigator has an opinion on the subject, each of which is subject to personal belief and inherent bias. For what it's worth, here's mine.

I first began investigating claims of the paranormal back in the mid-1990s, in my native Great Britain. I spent five years investigating claims of ghosts and hauntings across the U.K. before relocating to the United States. Over the course of those five years, I did not encounter even a single case that might be described as being demonic in nature. Few of them could even be considered particularly dark or frightening.

As the 21st century dawned, there came the advent of paranormal 'reality' TV, and with it came a veritable explosion of dark and demonic hauntings, most of which were long on scares, but short on actual facts.

Unfortunately, it didn't take long for the TV producer to figure out that the so-called 'demonic' episodes were the big ratings winners. TV viewers had no patience for stories of nice, friendly spirits; on the contrary, they wanted to see cases in which investigators were scratched, pushed, and best of all, possessed.

Obligingly, some of the TV shows delivered. Demons began cropping up everywhere on some of the more highly-dramatized shows, usually accompanied by sinister music and theories that often verged on the laughable.

The trend continues to this day on certain shows, to the point where one could be forgiven for thinking that there was a demonic entity lurking in practically every attic or basement.

I do not mean to give the impression that I don't believe in such things, although I prefer not to use the term 'demon,' which has very specific religious connotations. Nor am I disrespecting the beliefs of anybody. I remain very much open to the possibility of there being non-human entities, beings that have never walked the earth in human form. Conversations with my peers, extensive reading of the paranormal literature, not to mention several experiences during my own investigations in the United States, have all combined to make me believe that such entities are most probably out there. But I am convinced that they rear their heads far less frequently than some elements of the paranormal media would have us believe.

My friend Dave Schrader, host of the popular paranormal-themed shows *Darkness Radio* and *Midnight in the Desert*, once made a comment that has always stuck with me.

"I get a lot of people saying to me, 'Hey Dave, I think I have a demon in my house,'" he told me. "I always know that it's almost certainly not the case. You don't *think* you have a demon in your home. If you have a demon in your home, you *know* it for sure, because it's like a freight train ran through your life at full speed…"

Dave raises an excellent point. If the commonly-accepted view of such entities is correct, then their appearances are actually relatively few and far between, which is a good thing because according to those who have worked on such cases, the level of harm and destruction that comes in their wake is nothing short of devastating.

Which brings us back to the case of Denver Botanic Gardens.

There is nothing to suggest the presence of a demonic/non-human entity in this instance. Although some people have found the haunting to be frightening (an entirely understandable response to working on top of a graveyard) there have been no cases of harm being inflicted on anybody whatsoever that I am aware of.

Nothing about the history of the location, or the eyewitness testimony of those who work or visit there, suggests that there is an inhuman or demonic entity at work in this case.

It is my belief that we don't have to look very far to determine what exactly it is that haunts the gardens. The answer can be found just six feet beneath your feet.

The copier room seemed to be quite active, so we decided to stay in there a while longer. The photocopier itself made a few random noises, which were almost certainly part of its normal cycle of operation. Erik took the opportunity to ask whether the energy in the room had touched the copier at all. He wasn't really expecting an answer, but when we played back the remainder of the audio file, the sound of a whisper could be heard.

As an EVP, this would be categorized as a class C at best. This category of EVP is most likely anomalous in nature, but without clear and distinct words. In this case, the whisper had a somewhat feminine quality about it, but despite repeated listening with noise-canceling headphones, none of us could make out any specific words.

Still, it appeared that something in the copier room — the same something that Erik and Jill had sensed — wanted to make its presence known to us. It was Erik's impression that the unidentified entity wasn't really making an effort to hide itself. It was just hanging out, watching what we were doing and chiming in whenever it felt the urge to do so.

We ran a couple of short burst EVP sessions, playing them back immediately afterward through an external speaker.

"Let's keep it short," Erik said, kicking off the first burst. "No sense dragging this out."

I just couldn't help myself. "That's what my wife always says."

"Mine says 'Let's get this over with and watch TV,'" Erik deadpanned. We all cracked up. I wouldn't normally include something like this in a book, but amidst all the laughter at the crude joke, we all heard the sound of a loud gasp or chuckle. As with most EVPs, it sounded as if it had been overlaid on top of our conversation. It was almost as if a phantom voice was somehow piggybacking on our own words.

There was absolutely nothing feminine about *this* particular noise. It sounded almost like an asthmatic fighting for air, a choked gasp that may also perhaps have been a chuckle.

"It's getting cold over here," Richard said from his corner of the room. "I'm getting chills."

None of our equipment was measuring anything out of the ordinary.

Based upon this sensation, Richard took the lead during the next burst session, which took place in the hallway directly outside the copier room. Unfortunately, the session yielded no results.

"So much for the hallway," Richard said, shaking his head with disappointment. "Let's get back into the copier room again. That seems to be where all the action is."

Because we had recorded what we thought might have been a woman's voice in that room earlier on, I wondered aloud whether a female investigator might be able to establish some sort of connection or rapport with her. Jill stepped up to the plate and agreed to lead the session, which we were soon forced to cut short thanks to a hot-rodder driving past the building at high speed.

She had asked how many spirits were present, and

whether they were upset with the way that their graves had been treated. Once again, there was no answer. The only person who had gotten a response to his questions so far was Erik, so for our final session in the copier room, we put him back in the driver's seat.

When it became evident that he wasn't going to get any replies either this time, the rest of us all weighed in with our own questions, all in an effort to try and drum up some kind of activity.

It was all for nothing. The energy in the room had dissipated, the sensitives among us said, leaving the atmosphere feeling flat and empty. After getting some good initial results, things had deflated quickly.

"So much for that," Stephen said, doing his best to sound chipper. "What do you think we should do now?"

"We've tried high," Erik said, meaning that we had spent a lot of time on the upper floor. "How about we go low?"

Not having any better ideas, I nodded. "Alright then. Down to the basement we go."

The basement of the Waring House was as cold and unwelcoming as I remembered it being from our earlier visits, and it didn't surprise me in the least that some of the employees still didn't like to go down there, especially after dark. Normally I would have written that off as being nothing more than an overactive imagination, particularly when you thought about how many bodies lay just a few feet beneath the cement floor, but our past experiences down there had proven — to *my* satisfaction, at least — that the place was paranormally active.

Stephen and Erik were poring over a piece of ghost-hunting equipment that I wasn't familiar with. It was a metallic-looking box which, when Erik flipped the lid open, turned out to be mirrored inside on all six surfaces. The thing was small, no more than a couple of inches on each side, and a black electrical cable extended out of the box, terminating in a standard microphone jack.

"What's that?" I asked, fascinated with the little gadget.

"The Devil's Toybox," Erik replied, as if that explained everything. When I told him that I'd never heard of it, he said that the box was a live-EVP experimentation device, with an integrated piezoelectric microphone. The reflective sides were believed by some to form a cage that was capable of trapping spirits inside it.

"Trapping spirits?" I said, unable to disguise my abject

skepticism. "You don't seriously believe that, do you?"

"Not necessarily, but there's no harm in giving it a try."

I had seen a similar spirit-trapping experiment performed on one of the TV para-'reality' shows, and hadn't bought into it then. Nevertheless, I resolved to myself that if it really *did* seem that the box had ensnared a spirit entity — something I considered to be highly unlikely — we would adopt a catch-and-release policy. We had no business in trapping *anything* at the botanic gardens, assuming that such a thing was actually possible in the first place.

The use of mirrors for the purpose of spirit communication goes back many years, and the technique (most often known as *scrying*) is one that I have used on a number of my own investigations, with decidedly mixed results. In those cases, however, I have simply used a single mirror, rather than surrounding myself or the test subject with them.

Throughout folklore, reflective surfaces have long been associated with attempting to communicate with the dead. Many cultures have their own version of this particular concept. For example, I once worked with a paranormal investigator who was a Navajo. A highly-skilled and educated engineer by trade, not to mention being a skeptic with a superb ability to debunk all manner of supposedly paranormal phenomena, she nevertheless flatly refused to look in a mirror after dark, as beliefs ingrained in her during her upbringing maintained that evil spirits might be looking back at her from within the glass.

There's no real science behind the tenuous claim that such boxes can entrap spirit entities, though that doesn't necessarily mean that it isn't possible. If pushed to explain how mirrored boxes are supposed to work, the explanation is usually given that the reflective surfaces bounce energy around in a perpetual loop, thereby keeping it from escaping. If spirits really *can* use mirrors as some kind of gateway or portal into our own world, then the concept of a 'Devil's Toybox' would make for an intriguing possibility. Once again, as with so many aspects of the paranormal, unless there is some major scientific breakthrough, it all comes down to what you, as an individual, believe.

Personally, I was highly skeptical, but I agreed with Erik that there was no harm in trying the device and seeing what happened.

While Erik tinkered with his new toy, Stephen set up a Portal-style ITC device connected to his spirit box, which was in turn hooked up to an external speaker. Usually these devices work by amplifying the signal from a frequency-hopping radio and sometimes adding in optional reverberation. The basement was instantly flooded with fragments of voices, echoing from the walls and other surfaces. As usual, most of it was little more than gibberish, but I thought that it would be interesting to see whether some of the voices which had spoken to us in the basement previously would come through again.

It wasn't long before we heard something which none of us had ever heard come through a purported ITC device before: barking.

"What that a *dog*?" I asked, surprised.

"Sure sounds like it," Stephen agreed, his silhouette nodding in the near-total darkness. My mind went right back to the story of the phantom dog that Paula had told me during our earlier interview.

Coincidence, happenstance…or something more?

The barking, sadly, was to be the highlight of this particular session. Try as we might, we couldn't get anything even remotely intelligible to come through the speaker. If there were any intelligent spirits present, they were either unwilling or unable to interact with us.

"Hey!" The voice came from somewhere off to my left,

and sounded rather indignant. It turned out to be Richard, who told us all somewhat sheepishly that he had just felt something brush against his buttock. He was standing in a completely open space, away from any furniture or shelving, so there was nothing tangible that he could have caught himself on.

We were all disappointed that no real communication had occurred, but as far as Richard was concerned, it wasn't a complete wash. He was totally convinced that something had just touched him, and was quite pleased with this unexpected piece of physical phenomena.

"That's odd," Stephen said after switching on his flashlight. "My TASCAM voice recorder's dead."

"How long ago did you charge the battery?" Jill wanted to know.

"At the start of the investigation. It was right at one hundred percent. I think we're off to the races, ladies and gentlemen."

That was good news. Unexplained power drains were usually a fairly reliable indicator that something paranormal was afoot. It was a classic sign, one that was welcomed by investigators the world over.

"These things usually last for nine hours, at a

minimum," the priest said, shaking his head at the TASCAM. Then he raised his voice and spoke into thin air. "Well, wherever the energy went, you're welcome to use it to manifest."

"Feel free to take power from my devices too," Jill chimed in. "Whatever you need."

Now it was Erik's turn to get touched. No sooner had Jill spoken than the big man reached for the back pocket of his pants. We all looked at him quizzically.

"I have a flashlight in that back pocket," he explained, checking that it was still there. "It felt as though something just reached in and was *pushing* it downward."

"Look, this might sound like a crude joke," I began carefully, "but I promise you it isn't. I'll just come right out and say is: this is the second time in as many minutes that one of us got touched on the backside in here…"

Both of the investigators that this had happened to said that it felt playful and pranksterish, rather than intimidating. Erik pointed out that the body parts they had each been touched on would have been at exactly the right height for a mischievous child to have tapped them as he or she ran past. Our thoughts turned to the ghost of the young boy that was said to haunt the Waring House, the spirit we believed may have been responsible for startling Catlyn when she was in the restroom.

As theories went, it wasn't a bad one. I hadn't heard stories of any of the staff at the botanic gardens getting, for want of a better word, goosed, and thought it much more likely that we were dealing with an impish young lad than some kind of lascivious creeper.

After asking a few standard questions, which included requesting the identity of whoever had touched Richard and Erik and also who was responsible for draining the batteries in the audio recorder, we played back the audio. Gathering around the speaker expectantly, we were disappointed when the file finally came to an end and no apparent EVPs had been caught.

I sighed.

Those were the breaks.

CHAPTER ELEVEN
Roses

We spent a few more minutes lurking in the basement, asking questions but receiving no answers. Finally, we took the hint and returned to the main floor. Everybody was beginning to yawn, and so by mutual agreement, we took a ten-minute caffeine break. Munching on snacks, we discussed all that had happened so far, and debated what our next actions of the evening were going to be.

After the break was over, it was agreed that the more psychically-sensitive members of the team would go for a wander around the Waring House, trying to pick up traces of any energies that might be present, in much the same way that Erik had sensed something in the copier room earlier that night.

Our first stop was the kitchen, which the sensitives said felt flat and inert. Next was the top of the back staircase. Ditto for that.

Even the copier room showed no indication of the energies that my fellow investigators had picked up on earlier. Perhaps, I thought, the Waring House was just done with us for the night.

"That room is a possibility," Erik said, indicating the office space behind the locked door. "Too bad it's out of bounds."

Too bad indeed, but off limits meant off limits, and that was that. We went back downstairs again. As we passed by the main fireplace, I suddenly stopped dead in my tracks.

"Do you smell that?" I asked, wrinkling my nose.

"Smell what?" Erik asked from ten feet behind me.

"Something sweet and cloying...like perfume." I had walked head-first into what I can only describe as a wall of sweetness, something extremely aromatic (bordering on the pungent) which most definitely had not been there earlier on in the evening, when we had been unpacking our equipment in that very same room.

In fact, come to think of it, I realized that I hadn't smelled anything like it on *any* of our prior visits.

"Perfume, as in something a woman would wear?" Jill asked. "Or is it more of a cologne-type smell?"

Now that she mentioned it, I wasn't one hundred percent sure. I stood still for a moment and sniffed. The fragrance was still there, lingering in the background. Then, just as quickly, as if a switch had been thrown, it was gone.

Instantly, we began trying to debunk it. Nobody else had

smelled the aroma except for me. It had been immensely strong, and unmistakably real, or so I felt. The problem was, when just one person has an experience like that, it's difficult to classify it as proper evidence.

No matter how well-trained and well-intentioned an observer you may be, the human senses are very easily fooled. Every single one of our senses can be subject to hallucinations, given the proper circumstances, and given that none of my fellow investigators had smelled anything out of the ordinary, I could arrive at only one of three conclusions: either my nose was being fooled, I was imagining things…or something paranormal was afoot.

I was really hoping for the latter explanation to be true, but thanks to that inherent bias, I was determined to maintain an open mind. It was also good to be surrounded by a team of investigators who were willing to help me try and find a mundane explanation first.

Several sets of flowers had been placed all around the main lobby, some of which were artificial. Others were the real deal. Could I perhaps have been smelling the scent of those? If that had been the case, it should also have happened earlier on in the night. While it was possible that an errant breeze had suddenly wafted the smell over toward the fireplace, how then could we explain the fact that I was the only one who picked up on it — particularly when there were other investigators standing closer to the flowers than I was?

"I have an extremely sensitive nose," Erik pointed out. "It picks up scents pretty easily, and I haven't smelled anything like what you're describing in this room all night."

"And you were right behind me when I had the experience," I added. Indeed, Erik had only been a few steps to the back of me, and had come right to my side when I reported smelling the fragrance. I thought it was extremely unlikely that a natural odor could have dissipated so quickly.

Jill spotted another possible candidate, in the form of two candles which were sitting on top of the mantelpiece. Carefully, she took one of them down and sniffed it.

"It *does* have a pleasant smell," she admitted, placing it under my nose. "Is that what you smelled, Richard?"

I took several sniffs, and shook my head. "Not quite. Besides, look at the candles…they're still in their plastic wrappers. Only the wick at the top is exposed. There's not much of a gap for airborne particles to get through."

"Hey," Richard called out, trying to get our attention. "There's somebody walking around back here." He was standing in the lobby, and had just heard footsteps coming from somewhere behind him. When he went to check, not only was there nobody to be found, but the back and front doors to the house were both still locked, just as the security guards had left them.

It seemed as if, once again, we might have had invisible company.

"Richard, were you recording?" I asked, hoping that he had caught the footsteps. He shook his head. He had been playing back an audio recording at the time, reviewing it for potential EVPs. But he was adamant that he had heard the sound of footsteps and then somebody jiggling a doorknob, which once again brought back memories of Catlyn's restroom experience.

Perhaps our little friend was playing games with us once more.

While all of this excitement was going on, Stephen had not been idle. He had been sitting quietly at the top of the staircase, running a digital voice recorder and trying to attune himself with the spirits of the Waring House.

This was something he often did when we investigated

together. When there is a lot of hustle and bustle going on, it can sometimes be difficult for those with psychic sensitivities to get an accurate reading on the various energies that they wish to tune into — the 'background noise' tends to drown them out. Getting away from the crowd and placing himself in a dark and quiet spot was one of Stephen's favorite techniques for overcoming that.

He had started a spirit box running at a low volume and after getting himself settled, the priest had begun to ask questions.

"Can you tell me my name?"

Steve, the box replied instantly.

He was impressed, to say the least.

That was the only intelligible response that he received during the entire session. Finally, after spending a quarter of an hour without having any luck, he decided to take the hint.

"If you guys aren't going to talk to me, then I'm just going to leave," he said, reaching for the spirit box.

BYE! it boomed out at him.

"Okay, okay, I'm going…"

He came back downstairs to re-join the rest of the group. We wasted no time in filling him in on the details of what had just happened to us. Stephen listened intently without interruption, then helped himself to a drink of water while we all pondered our next move.

As he wandered from the lobby into the main hall to join Richard in the near corner, Stephen stopped dead in his tracks — exactly the same reaction that I had had when I walked past the fireplace.

"Okay, now *I'm* smelling perfume," he said, frowning.

"I smell it too," Richard added. "It's almost like a rose bush."

"Yes!" I agreed, glad that he had put a name to what it was that I had smelled. It had indeed reminded me of roses, but I couldn't quite find the words to describe it.

This unexpected turn of events made me feel extremely happy. Here was apparent validation of something that, I had begun to worry, may have been nothing more than my mind playing tricks on me. While I could accept the possibility of that quite easily, what were the odds of *three* of us experiencing an olfactory hallucination? No, whatever we were smelling was objectively real, and there was nothing that we could find to explain it.

"I'm wondering if what we're smelling is the perfume of a female spirit," Jill suggested. "Maybe the lady whose voice we heard upstairs."

It was a plausible theory. We were now seriously considering the possibility that the fun-loving child's spirit had been playing games with us earlier on, touching the two investigators downstairs in the cellar, and that the female might be keeping a closer eye on us while we were on the upper two floors.

Fifteen minutes passed without anything significant happening. Then it was Jill and Erik's turn to experience exactly the same thing, in exactly the same area. They were chatting about nothing in particularly, when suddenly there it was: the smell of roses.

We practically tore the fireplace and its surrounding environs apart, trying to find some natural explanation. Once again, we turned up empty-handed. Then just as quickly as it had arrived, the aroma was gone again.

It was maddening, frustrating, and fascinating in equal measure.

What to do next? After a little discussion, we settled upon a burst EVP session on the hidden staircase. Taking up positions from the top to the bottom of the staircase, we sat down carefully, to the accompaniment of many groans and creaks from the wooden steps and our own middle-aged bodies.

Jill led off, and the theme of the session was to try and contact the lady of the house. After asking a series of respectful questions concerning the house, the grounds, and their history, Jill played back the audio file and I recorded the replay.

"Listen," she said, after hearing her own voice ask how many spirits there were in the area. "I'll play it again."

This time, we all heard it…the sound of a child, giggling.

"Could it have been some random person, just wandering across Cheesman Park?" I asked, ever the skeptic.

"It's possible," she admitted. But the voice had sounded a little too young for that, and we hadn't heard much in the way of outside noise interference while sitting on the back staircase.

A loud, automated bleeping noise caught our attention. It was coming from the direction of the lobby. We would find out later that it was coming from a motion sensor that was set up in one of the smaller anterooms facing the restroom, an office that belonged to the receptionist. The interesting thing was that it was located behind a closed door, begging the question of what exactly might have triggered it.

It wasn't long until sunrise. We were all getting tired, running mostly on caffeine and adrenaline. The yawns were coming thick and fast from all sides of the table, a sure sign that it was getting close to the time for calling it a night. I called the security hotline while the rest of the team finished packing up their equipment.

A few minutes later, the back door opened, admitting two security guards. Standing in the main hall, Stephen and I watched in astonishment as one of the doors at the opposite end of the room swung open, creaking in the most sinister way imaginable. The doors led into the events room, home to the concealed back staircase, and had stayed closed all night…until now.

"That's wild," Stephen said.

"The timing's suspicious," I pointed out. It was, in fact, *perfect* timing for the door to have opened itself, and in the field of paranormal research, if something looks too good to be true, then it usually is. Introducing myself to the two somewhat bemused security guards, I asked if they'd be willing to help us out with a little experiment. They were kind enough to agree. Stephen closed the door once again, returning it to the same position as it had been in before.

I asked the security guards to step outside and come in once again, in exactly the same way that they had entered before — opening the back door of the house with the same amount of force. Shrugging, they obliged us. Stephen and I watched and tried to conceal our disappointment as the events room door opened itself once again.

There were two possible explanations. The change in air pressure introduced by the back door being opened could have pushed the other door open (there was an air flow-path between the two doors, albeit with a ninety-degree bend in between them both); alternatively, the vibration of the back door opening and hitting the wall could have transmitted through the walls and floor of the building itself and given the events room door a gentle nudge — just enough to push it open.

Whichever explanation turned out to be the case (and it could have been a combination of the two) there was nothing paranormal about the events room door seeming to open of its own accord. Which was a shame, because it had looked spectacular at first, but I was satisfied that we had found a plausible, totally non-paranormal reason behind it.

It was a good debunk, and despite the slight sense of disappointment that came along with it, we ended the night on a high note.

As they locked us out of the Waring House, I asked Park and Travis, the two security guards, whether they had experienced anything strange there themselves. One hadn't, and the other said that he had heard quite a few stories.

"I've heard two separate stories from two different guards who started working here and then quit on the spot," he told us. "One just heard about the haunting here and left. The other one experienced something that frightened him so much, he hung it up. Didn't want to deal with it anymore."

One of the security guards who had trained them had worked at the botanic gardens for almost nine years, and swore that one night, he had seen a bright white light shining down from one of the upstairs windows in the Waring House after he had locked the place up for the night. What made this even more unusual was that the light was perfectly square. The senior security guard apparently decided that discretion was the better part of valor, as he never went back inside to find out what it was.

I looked up at those same windows as we walked away, half-expecting to see the white square of light myself.

Instead, the only thing looking back at me was reflected light from the outside.

Returning to our cars, the AAPI crew and I said our goodbyes and went our separate ways. It had been quite the night, with an interesting mix of tactile and audible phenomena. There was one more night remaining in my investigation of the Waring House, and I was eager to find out what the spirits had in store for us.

CHAPTER TWELVE
Just Shut Up

This was it: our final night of the investigation.

A week had passed, and things were ramping up at the botanic gardens. Halloween was right around the corner, and it wouldn't be long before a slew of visiting members of the public started reporting their own otherworldly encounters to the staff.

We chose a Saturday night this time, and once again started at ten o'clock. I was accompanied by fellow investigators Jason, Linda, Randy, and Robbin. We were delighted to be joined once more by Stephen, Erik, and Jill, giving us a full compliment of veteran paranormal investigators. (Sadly, Richard was unable to make it).

I was hoping for a strong finish to what had been a fascinating field research project so far.

As non-sensitives, Jason, Linda, and I were in the minority. Once the security guards had locked us inside the Waring House once again, I asked Robbin whether she was picking up on anything. "It feels very heavy in here," she said right away. The other sensitives agreed, which I wanted to take as a good sign: hopefully an indicator that we would have company that night.

Our investigation began in what we had taken to calling the dining room, thanks to its ornately-carved wooden table and associated furnishings. Setting up our equipment on the tabletop, we each took a seat around the table itself and got ready to kick off the night with an EVP session.

"Oh, what the…" Linda was frowning. Some of her equipment, which she had spent all day charging to maximum capacity, appeared to be dead already. We had only been inside the building for fifteen minutes, and already the unexplained power drains had started.

Each investigator began to position their various sensors, and then fired up the equipment they had brought. I had gone with an Ovilus and a pair of digital voice recorders. The atmosphere was casual and informal, as it usually was, because the investigation hadn't properly started yet. We laughed and joked amongst ourselves, enjoying what basically amounted to a reunion of old friends in a *very* cool haunted location.

Unable to help myself, I made a pretty weak joke, earning myself a groan from everybody. I leaned into the digital voice recorder and said, "Note to self: remove that from the book!"

Instantly the Ovilus said, *REMOVE*.

The laughter stopped instantly. *Wow*, I thought, looking around the table. *Either that's one hell of a coincidence, or…*

Score another hit for the Ovilus.

After some discussion, we agreed upon a spirit box session in the dining room. Our instrument of choice was the newer SB-11 box, rather than the older SB-7, which some investigators swore was more reliable, despite its need for an external speaker.

All of the lights were switched off, leaving the room as dark as we could get it. Only the ambient light from the lobby outside and whatever came through the frosted windows prevented us from being in complete blackness.

While the rest of us were gathered around the table, Jill tucked herself into one of the corners so that she could cover as much of the room as possible with the SLS camera.

The Ovilus was left running, and kicked off our session by saying the word *DYING*.

"Hello!" Erik called out cheerfully. "Can you say hello to us through the radio?"

Ten seconds later, a female voice responded through the SB-11:

Demon.

We looked at one another with raised eyebrows. There was that word again...

The SB-11 was cycling through radio frequencies, hopping from one to the next quicker than the ear could detect. The d-word, as I liked to call it, was the only intelligible word that came out of it, in between bursts of static, white noise, and snippets from local radio stations.

"What's the name of the gentleman I'm pointing to?" I asked, indicating Stephen.

Stupid, responded the SB-11, almost exactly on cue. The good-natured priest burst into laughter, taking no offense at the apparent insult.

Hot on the heels of that, the box said the word, *JASON,* which once again challenged the boundaries of coincidence just a little too much for my liking. This was the first time that the SB-11 had named one of the investigators directly, and we found that to be a very encouraging development — at first.

But another thirty minutes' worth of questioning yielded nothing whatsoever of any value. It was as if the voices had popped up just long enough to insult Stephen, say hello to Jason, and then disappeared again, leaving us with nothing more than static.

More than a little disappointed, we powered down the spirit box, thinking that it was time to change things up a little.

Unbeknownst to us, however, Jill was about to get something of a shock.

"Hey!" she said, sounding startled. All eyes turned toward her. She was staring wide-eyed at the screen of the SLS camera. She went on to explain that she been scanning us all with the camera, pacing around the perimeter of our circle and making as little noise as possible. Suddenly, she sensed movement through the open doorway, and swung the SLS around to face it.

Standing there in the lobby was a human-shaped stick figure, one that was at least six feet tall when judged in relation to its surroundings. As quickly as it had appeared, the mysterious figure vanished from the SLS screen.

Who, we wondered, was our elusive watcher?

Remaining at the table, Stephen asked whether one of our unseen companions could make a loud noise. I don't think that he was seriously expecting an answer, which made it all the more surprising when it came in the form of a whistle coming from somewhere inside the house.

"Could you tell me your name?" he asked.

PAUL, responded the Ovilus.

A colossal rumbling sound, loud and very near, caused some of us to nearly jump out of our skin. After just a moment, we realized that it was nothing more than thunder, albeit very close to the house. It was accompanied by a brilliant white flash that lit up the entire room for a split-second, throwing our long black shadows up against the walls and windows.

How perfect — we were investigating a haunted house at night and in the middle of a thunderstorm. What could possibly go wrong?

We finished the burst session and played it back. Just as Stephen finished asking for any spirits present to tell him their name, there was a whisper...faint, indistinct, but most definitely *there*.

Linda put on her noise-cancelling headphones and listened to it repeatedly, but try as she might, she could not make out the specific words that were being spoken. Nevertheless, we could say with confidence that none of the investigators present had whispered anything during the EVP session. Chalk up a Class C-bordering-on-D EVP, not the most impressive of evidence perhaps, but no less interesting for that. The timing seemed more than coincidental, coming as it did right after Stephen had asked a question.

Encouraged by what was apparently an attempt to communicate, we chose to stay in the dining room for a while longer and try a different piece of equipment. Randy was eager to run his Phasma Box, and the rest of us were interested to see what results it might produce.

He cranked up the volume on his laptop, and the sound of distorted voices began to reverberate around the room.

Stephen began asking questions. When no answers were forthcoming, he went around the table, indicating each different investigator and asking if somebody could name them. Again, no response. A slightly exasperated Stephen asked if he should just shut up, to which a salty female voice replied, *Just shut up!*

The team broke into laughter. He had asked for an answer, and there it was.

"Fine, fine," Stephen raised his hands in mock surrender. "Somebody else's turn."

Linda began asking about the identity of the spirits in the basement. From just outside in the lobby, there came the sound of footsteps. Jason went out to check on the source, wondering if the security guards had entered the building, but the whole area was completely empty.

As the session wore on, I began to wonder whether the *just shut up* wasn't just directed at Stephen specifically, as he had first thought. *Nothing* intelligent was coming through the Phasma Box at all, from what I could hear — after those first encouraging occurrences, we were now drawing a blank.

"Let's split up," Jill suggested. That seemed like a great idea to me. Some of the investigators went down to the basement, closing the heavy door behind them in order to minimize noise contamination.

Wanting to extend them the same courtesy, Robbin, Jill, and I chose the back staircase, which was at the opposite end of the house. Although we had learned during past visits that sound could still carry from one end of the building to the other, thanks to some rather strange acoustics, we could mitigate that a little bit by keeping our voices down to a hushed and respectable level.

The three of us took up positions on the staircase, with myself at the bottom, Jill halfway up, and Robbin at the top, where she disappeared into the darkness of the upper landing once the lights were switched out. This time out, we stuck to the basic tools — recorders, flashlights, and EMF meters.

Jill led off with the questioning in a one-minute burst, and although no voices registered on the recording when we played it back, we did hear two loud and very distinct knocks immediately after she asked for anybody present to tell us a little something about themselves. They came from somewhere up above our heads. We immediately set about trying to debunk the knocks. The first and most obvious explanation would be the pipes, but we had heard nothing like it during any of our other sessions on the back staircase before.

Next, we looked at the possibility of them having originated downstairs in the basement. Perhaps, I suggested, this was simply noise contamination. After the session, I checked with the basement team and confirmed that they had not been knocking at all during the course of their own experiments.

Now it was Robbin's turn to take over the questioning. She introduced herself politely, and asked how many spirit people were with us. In response, a single, clear knock sounded from inside the wall off to her right.

"Okay," she said to herself. "Just one of you. Could you please bang again?"

The noise which seemed to reply to her came from

halfway up the staircase, closer to Jill.

Robbin looked down at the Ovilus. She had switched off the audible voice mode, in order to prevent more noise contamination from being introduced into the environment. As energy levels on the staircase changed, the Ovilus now output its words directly onto the digital screen that was built into the device.

"Can you show yourself, perhaps as a light form?" Robbin requested.

CANNOT, the Ovilus responded.

"Interesting…" Robbin thought about it for a moment. "I asked if you could appear to us…is this is your way of telling me that you can't?"

Another knock, this one louder and more distinct than the rest.

"Then could you please call out to us as loud as you possibly can?"

There was no response to her request this time. There were no further knocks, no matter what Robbin asked. I tried asking questions myself, but the source of the knocking had evidently gone quiet.

After thirty minutes had gone past, the groups all congregated in the main hall to compare notes. Linda noted that the heavy door downstairs had creaked open by itself on two separate occasions, and she had seen a black shape pass by the gap between the door and the frame, which seemed to have impressed her. Unfortunately, she was the only observer, and so without a corroborating eyewitness, it was tough to call it evidence.

The odor of perfume had also been smelled down in the basement — shades of our fireplace experience on our last visit — and both Erik and Randy had seen a flash of light at about the same time. Ordinarily, this is something that he would have written off as simply being a car headlight or something equally mundane…except for the fact that there were no windows in the basement room that they were conducting their EVP session in.

As the old saying goes, 'speak of the Devil and he's sure to appear.' The floral/perfume-like smell that had plagued us the week before was back, and stronger than ever. We could all smell it, close to the fireplace. It hadn't been there all evening, and we had passed back and forth countless times without smelling it. And now, at 1:45am, there it was again.

Then just like that, it was gone. We tried yet again to debunk it, quickly dismissing the shrink-wrapped candles and the flowers that were easily thirty feet away in the lobby, and could not find a satisfactory explanation for it.

CHAPTER THIRTEEN
WE SAW HER

We had been going for four hours by now, and the best evidence so far had come from the back staircase and the basement. After a quick discussion, we all voted to go back down to the basement for another ITC session.

This time, Stephen wanted to use his Specterceiver, a device I wasn't very familiar with. As he started setting it up, Stephen explained that this was a piece of software which used a dictionary of reverse phonetic words from the Korean and Russian languages as its base lexicon. Spirit entities can allegedly switch those phonetic words around, changing them into English words and phrases in order to communicate with the operator.

The technical explanation for the way this device was supposed to work was, frankly, above my head. But I wasn't beyond trying out any tool or technique that might yield results, within reason. While Stephen fiddled with the phone app, I settled myself down on the cold basement floor and leaned back against the wall to watch.

I was chatting with Robbin about nothing much in particular, when all of a sudden, I felt something tap me firmly on the left shoulder. I looked in her direction and asked if it had been her.

"No," she insisted, "I didn't touch you."

She was sitting a good eight feet away from me. There was no way she could have covered that distance quickly enough to tap me on the shoulder and then get back to her starting position without being seen, either by me or by somebody else. Nobody had seen her move, and besides, she isn't the sort of person to play pranks on a paranormal investigation in the first place. In over a decade of investigating with her, I have never seen her play a practical joke once. Indeed, while we are not averse to making verbal jokes, the rules of both our research groups expressly forbid pranking of any sort.

It was a very distinct tap. I hadn't imagined it, and I hadn't brushed against anything on my left-hand side either. This was the same room in which both Richard and Erik had gotten touched on the behind the week before, and I wondered whether it was the same playful spirit — perhaps that of the little boy.

"Did somebody just tap Richard on the shoulder?" Robbin asked, to which the Specterceiver immediately replied, *Yes*.

There is something deeply personal about getting physically touched by something that you cannot see. As a paranormal investigator, it's easy to get blaise and jaded when it happens to other people all around you, but when it finally happens to you, the feeling is a very visceral reminder that the inexplicable phenomena you are dealing with is all too real.

Me and Robbin, the Specterceiver said, in a guttural male voice.

"Oh wow," Randy said, looking over at his wife. We had no idea what the sentence had meant, but Robbin's name was easy to hear.

"What do you want to do with Robbin?" Stephen asked.

Everything.

"Uh oh." Robbin was taking it in her stride. She'd been the focus of similar comments coming through spirit boxes during past investigations, and even though they made her feel a little uncomfortable, she always maintained a sense of humor.

Object of my desire, was the next statement.

"Maybe it's talking about *you*, Richard," Robbin joked with a mischievous twinkle in her eye.

"Which one do you prefer?" Randy asked the speaker.

"Robbin or Richard?"

HELP!

The team started laughing at the somewhat bizarre turn the ITC session had taken. The responses, seemingly intelligent in nature, were coming thick and fast now, right on the heels of the questions. The same harsh-sounding male voice delivered each answer promptly and with an apparent lack of emotion.

Estep, the male voice whispered. That one sent a chill running through me. Being personally singled out by what may or may not have been a discarnate entity was more than a little creepy, no matter how seasoned a paranormal investigator you might be.

Fortunately for me, I wasn't to be the only one. *Jill* was next, once again spoken in a hushed whisper. Jill raised an eyebrow but said nothing.

"Who are the other people here?" Stephen asked.

Stephen.

"That's right! How about this guy?" Stephen pointed at Randy.

Ask Richard.

"What's my name?" Randy called out.

There was no answer. We all noticed that the air was

getting colder down there in the basement filing room, something that Randy verified with a thermometer.

"I keep getting the feeling that there's somebody standing behind me," Stephen said, clutching his arms to himself in an attempt to warm himself up. "It's *so* cold in here!"

Standing closer to the doorway, both Jill and Robbin reported feeling a very strange tingling sensation. While a completely subjective phenomenon, I found it interesting that they both noted the sensation independently of one another. It was something to be filed under 'interesting, but not evidence.'

"Are you okay if we try a different means of communication?" Stephen enquired. There followed a long silence, and then an almost sullen, *Yeah.*

Stephen shut down the Specterceiver and Randy switched over to the Phasma Box. While he was finalizing the setup, Stephen asked Robbin who the woman was that was standing behind her — the priest explained that he was sensing a female presence back there, and Robbin agreed with him. She was getting a very similar impression.

We saw her, the Phasma Box chimed in.

"Can you give us the name of somebody who is buried

beneath us?" Randy wanted to know.

No.

Just then, we all heard the sound of footsteps walking on the hard floor outside the room, close to the base of the stairs. Robbin pushed the door open. The footsteps stopped instantly. Nobody was out there. Completely fearless, the diminutive investigator went out there, walking directly towards the position where we had last heard the footsteps. Jill was right behind her, to provide a second set of eyes in case she saw something out of the ordinary.

That was real, a voice from the Phasma Box insisted.

I was interested in trying to learn more about this potential spirit communicator. "Are you by any chance Catholic? Would prayers help?"

In the basement.

"So, prayers would help you?" I said again, to which a female voice, new to the conversation, responded with, *possible*. "Would you like us to say some prayers? We have a Catholic priest with us."

SAY IN ENGLISH! It was the same female voice.

Things had taken a fascinating turn. Rather than say prayers in Latin, it seemed that whoever was talking wanted them to be said in plain English instead. Stephen agreed that when we wrapped up our investigation on what would be our final night, he would perform a brief Catholic ceremony of prayer, in an attempt to help whichever souls might benefit from it.

Now the male voice was back: *Richard,* was all he said. His was followed by an entirely new male voice, which said quite clearly, *How's the investigation?*

The session was beginning to get rather impressive.

There was a loud thump. Randy turned around. It sounded as if something had just struck one of the cardboard boxes full of files that sat on a shelf behind him, though none of them were away from their original position from what he could see.

INCOMING! said a female voice via the Phasma Box.

"Ow, hey!" Robbin jerked forward, reaching behind her with one hand. Something had just jabbed her in the small of the back. This wasn't the kind of playful swat that Richard, Erik, and I had all experienced down there in that same room. This was something more forceful. It may not have been unfriendly, however — rather than being meant to inflict pain, it could simply have been the entity's only way of making its presence known.

"That wasn't a touch," she winced, rubbing her back

slowly. "That was a full-on *poke!*"

"Can you do that again, please?" Randy was asking politely, rather than challenging. We weren't willing to be confrontational in a place like this, where any spirit entities were most likely of the misunderstood and hard-done-by variety, rather than the overtly malicious kind. His request was not to be fulfilled, however, and over the course of the next fifteen minutes, the intelligent communications through the Phasma Box stopped coming. This isn't at all unusual; it is almost as if there is a limited window for communication, and once it closes, it is closed for an undefined period of time before opening up again later on. It may also be that there is a finite amount of energy available, which must be recharged in some way before communication and physical manifestations can again take place.

Reluctantly, we picked up our equipment and headed back upstairs to the main hall. Things were starting to wind down for the night, and I wanted to get in at least one more session before the security staff came to lock up.
The flowery aroma completely filled the lobby and most of the main hall when we came back upstairs. We had no more luck figuring out the cause than before. I even started looking around for those automatic air freshener units, the

type that emit a spray every few minutes on a timed cycle. Needless to say, I didn't find any.

This was going to be our last session at the botanic gardens. By mutual agreement, we settled on what we all thought was the most active part of the Waring House: the copier room.

It was quite a squeeze, getting all of us in there, but somehow, we managed. Erik was the first to ask questions, due to his strong track record of getting evidence in the copier room. When the recording of his session came back empty, Robbin took over. She stuck to basic everyday questions. When her burst was over, Linda asked whether anybody had heard an additional voice during the session. We all shook our heads to indicate that we had not.

"Play back the audio then," Linda said, "because I know what I heard."

Eagerly, we gathered around the speaker and listened.

"I'm going to the store," Robbin's recorded voice could be heard to say. "Does anybody want anything?"

A woman's voice, faint but definitely there, whispered, I DO.

We played it back several times to make sure, finally concluding that this was a direct voice. Unlike the standard

EVP, which is not heard at the time of recording, this answer had been witnessed by Linda, which made it a prime example of the direct voice phenomenon.

That wasn't all. As Robbin asked, "Is there anything that you want to say to anyone in this room?", an indecipherable muttering or whispering could be heard on the recording. None of us had heard anything like it at the time, and none of us were speaking. Nor was anybody passing by on the street outside — we were watching to make sure.

Once again, we had captured (and in Linda's case, actually heard with her own ears) the sound of a woman speaking to us in the copier room. These weren't residual sounds, because the timing was too apropos. These were intelligent responses to our questions, recorded on multiple occasions in the same place. We can only conclude that a female entity still haunts that particular part of the Waring House.

As to her identity, we could not say. Perhaps she was a former lady of the house, or alternatively she may have been one of the thousands who was buried in Mount Calvary Cemetery and whose bones still lie undiscovered beneath the Waring House to this day.

We may not have positively identified her, but simply

confirming the truth of her existence was a very satisfying end to our investigation.

Someday, we hope that she will talk to us again.

AFTERWORD

I have spent a great deal of time thinking about the Gardens haunting.

When we consider the history of the land itself, particularly in light of the fact that so many sets of human remains were either desecrated or simply grassed over and forgotten, it is easy to see why many of those poor souls may not be resting in peace.

During its heyday, the old Mount Prospect/Mount Calvary cemetery was the burial ground for Catholics, Hebrews, and numerous other faiths. Sections were devoted to the burial of Chinese immigrants, soldiers from the Grand Army of the Republic, Oddfellows, Masons, and both the rich and the penniless alike.

Looking at a map of the original cemetery today, overlaid with a Denver street grid, it is plain to see that both the Waring House and the conservatory are built squarely atop the Catholic section. The most active nights of our investigation were the final two, and it occurs to me with the benefit of hindsight that those were the nights when we were accompanied by a Catholic priest.

Taking that particular train of thought a little bit further, let's look back at the second night, which was our first evening in the Waring House. Things were extremely quiet, with the exception of Stan and Seth capturing an EVP down in the basement…moments after Stan had said, *"In nomine Patris et Filii et Spiritus Sanctii,"* a Latin blessing well-known to members of the Catholic church.

Is it mere coincidence that the best results seemed to occur when there was some kind of Catholic connection? My advice to future paranormal investigators at the Waring House is to take along a Bible, crucifix, and other Christian articles, as it may assist you in making contact with the resident spirits there.

Broadly speaking, there are two categories of haunting: residual and intelligent. Residual hauntings are the paranormal equivalent of video tapes or movie files on a computer: moments in time that were captured by some type of mechanism which we currently do not fully understand, and can then be played back when the circumstances (and perhaps more importantly, the eyewitnesses) are right. There is no intelligence or disembodied personality present, *per se*. These hauntings are no more alert or self-aware than the people that you see on your TV screen.

Intelligent hauntings, on the other hand, will interact

with the living. They will answer questions, move objects or make noises (sometimes on request) and even touch you at times. In these instances, we are dealing with some kind of discarnate intelligence. Whether you believe that we are dealing with the spirits of the dead, a non-human entity, or even a person from a different time or dimension, the key point is that there is a distinct personality at work here.

Hauntings are not necessarily comprised entirely of one type or another. Often there is a mix of both kinds.

The Denver Botanic Gardens haunting is, in my opinion, primarily an intelligent one, with a dash of residual activity on the side. Most of the phenomena which my team and I encountered — being touched, having our questions answered via direct voice and by EVP, the restroom door being rattled — all appear to be intelligent. The unexplained smells, on the other hand, seem more residual in nature, though it is, of course, impossible to say for sure.

The staff at Denver Botanic Gardens live, for the most part, quite happily with their otherworldly predecessors. While there is a degree of nervousness and even fear at times, most of those who work there love their jobs and love their place of employment. Long may it remain so.

Yet as time goes on, the Waring House will continue to

sink, as more coffins rupture in their earthern cavities. Subsidence will gradually worsen. Bones will continue to be disturbed. More human remains will be accidentally unearthed.

Who knows what will happen to the levels of paranormal activity then? What should the employees do?

I, for one, hope that the first thing they will do is give me a call...

Acknowledgments

Firstly, to you, the reader: Thank you for spending your hard-earned money and valuable time in order to read this book. It is my sincere hope that you have enjoyed it, and would ask you to please consider rating the book on Amazon's website. In the current writing market, books tend to live and die by their reviews and ratings, particularly on Amazon. Your help would therefore be greatly appreciated.

Some other thanks are due to the people without whom this book would not have been possible.

A special thank-you to the staff of Denver Botanic Gardens (most especially **Tiffany Coleman**) for allowing us access to research the haunting, and for supporting this book project since its inception.

Laura, for her constant support.

My partners-in-crime **Linda** and **Jason Fellon, Catlyn Keenan, Stephen Weidner, Erik Bensen, Richard Ricketts, Jill Woodward Saunderson, Seth Woodmansee, Jennifer Hirzel, Shane Rogers, Randy Schneider,** and

Robbin Daidone for investigating the Denver Botanic Gardens haunting alongside me.

Paula Vanderbilt and **Rose Glenn** for sharing their experiences with me.

My **Asylum 49** family, still running the greatest haunt on the planet. Love you all.

My brothers and sisters at **AMR Boulder, Golden,** and **Longmont,** not to mention **Boulder Rural Fire.**

If you feel so inclined, please visit me over at my web page, **www.richardestep.net.** I love to hear from readers, so drop by and say hi!

Much love,
Richard

The Waring House (Shane Rogers)

The front door of 909 York Street (Shane Rogers)

The author investigating in the lobby (Shane Rogers)

The table at which we conducted our EVP sessions (Shane Rogers)

Robbin taking a break in the Great Hall (Shane Rogers)

The bells ring with no human contact (Shane Rogers)

The lobby (Shane Rogers)

Jason, Catlyn, and the author poring over a map of the cemetery that lies beneath the Gardens (Shane Rogers)

The author lifting the hinged staircase (Shane Rogers)

An ebullient Catlyn investigating the hidden crawlspace beneath the staircase (Shane Rogers)

Employees are asked to keep the basement door closed and latched because "it keeps the ghosts in!" (Shane Rogers)

Robbin, Randy, and the author discussing what to do next (Shane Rogers)

The restroom door which caused Catlyn a great deal of consternation (Shane Rogers)

Printed in Great Britain
by Amazon